Art & Inquiry

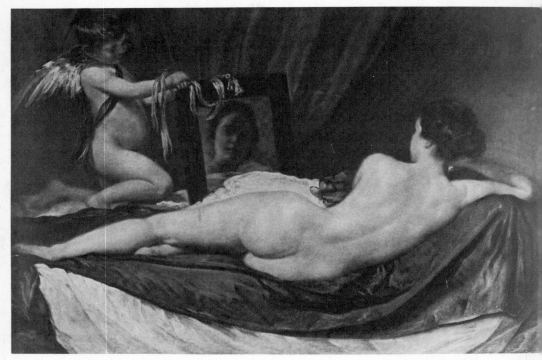

Velasquez, *The Rokeby Venus* (courtesy of the National Gallery, London).

The work of art . . . is essentially a question. . . .
Hegel

Our datum is the actual world, including ourselves.
A. N. Whitehead

Art & Inquiry

by Berel Lang

University of Colorado

Wayne State University Press
Detroit, 1975

Contents

Introduction

In the essays that make up this volume, I try first to say what the work of aesthetics is and then to do some of it. Apologies before the act, I know, will sound disingenuous; but they may be less suspect if they only acknowledge the contrast which inevitably marks aesthetic theory and the fact that it is not itself the art about which it speaks. More sharply than any other part of philosophical inquiry, aesthetics reveals a disparity between its own results and the objects of its analysis. There are few enterprises which so willfully "murder to dissect."

This contrast, however, despite its appeal to common sensibility, is invidious. Aesthetics has its place (for those who leave it any place at all) within the boundaries of philosophy; we should not be surprised, then, to find that it is not art. Undoubtedly its advocates have some obligation to defend the venture of speculative understanding, as the conclusions of aesthetic inquiry diverge from the more obvious uses or pleasures of doing and making. This burden of defense belongs not to aesthetics alone, however, but to philosophical practice in general; if aesthetics as a project is not farther from reproach than other parts of the enterprise of philosophy, its formal claims to respectability are hardly more dubious than theirs.

An analogous response can be made to the charge that the work of aesthetics moves in a circle—that it starts from the identification of certain features of experience from which its investigators hope to extract the principles or structure that are required to identify those features in the first place. This problem is inescapable for the work of philosophy: there, if anywhere, we recognize that the world of understanding is not moved by any lever external to it. But if this is true in general, the only possible response to such charges—that not all circles are vicious—is, again, one which is not peculiarly the responsibility of the writer on aesthetics.

How is it then that this manner of innocence should be so harshly indicted? For we have heard regularly of the "dreariness of aesthetics," that "aesthetics does not begin to exist." Almost certainly, I think the answer must be, because the manner itself has been unclear in design. The objections are often conceded by aestheticians themselves, for example, that aesthetics says little about the actual appearances of art in its historical occurrence, that the conclusions of aesthetics fail to reflect the immediacy of art. But these are gratuitous professions of guilt by dissociation: it was never the purpose of the work of aesthetics to imitate art or to reconstruct its history. Indeed what the writing of aesthetics lacks in much of its contemporary expression is not sensitivity to the moments of art or adequacy in their representation so much as philosophical coherence; a grasp of the speculative texture of the questions generated by the phenomenon of art, not of the techniques of perception or production. The need for such techniques is obvious enough; but it is not at all clear that this need ought to (or could) be met by aesthetic theory.

The most substantial encumbrances on the work of aesthetics have explicitly, even deliberately, been of its own making, due to its *philosophical* indispositions. It is difficult to know, for example, what might have been expected of attempts to isolate the analysis of critical judgment from that of the work of art; of attempts to treat the experience related to art aside from the estimates of other experience, or to lay the ground for a reconstruction of aesthetic objects with no reference to the structure of *other* objects. Yet the literature of aesthetics includes many such efforts and has suffered proportionately, even in its attempts to communicate the most immediate qualities of art.

Again, on another side, we find the new philosophical methodologist stocking his museum of antiquities and eccentricities with the logical and linguistic confusions of which traditional aesthetics—like the dogmatic metaphysics of which it was allegedly a symptom—(also allegedly) made free. "Every thing is what it is," we are reminded by G. E. Moore, as though either the present or past had suffered a dearth of tautologies, "and not another thing." And surely what is needed in aesthetics in order that the last moral be drawn from this critique is not a more responsive sensibility to the actual moments of art or even to the talk about them (valuable as these would be) but some part of the inspiration that animates traditional philosophy for comprehending those appearances, for locating their grounds. The tradition of that need, at least, remains constant.

Such reflections on the recent past of aesthetic inquiry promise more for its immediate future than prudence warrants. At any rate, I hardly attempt here to set everything right. I am concerned principally with the lineage and systematic structure of several characteristic issues of aesthetics. These issues, it will become evident, are separable rather than separate; the relations among them comprise a formal pattern within the bounds of aesthetics and define a particular strategy for its work. After the discussion of this pattern in chapter 1, I focus in the later essays on a sequence of individual issues, the formulations of which originate in what I take to be a preponderance of concrete aesthetic and extra-aesthetic evidence. The later discussion thus moves into a number of the principal areas of philosophical inquiry: into value theory with its implications for critical judgment, into epistemology as it bears on the problems of the denotation and truth of art, and finally (a once and future caveat) into metaphysics as it purports to afford a grasp of the aesthetic process as such.

The method used in the inquiry is, in a restricted sense, transcendental. The enterprise of aesthetics presupposes, the argument here asserts, the discrimination of certain moments of experience which serve, historically and systematically, as a ground. The character of this ground governs the philosophical inquiry which emerges from it: the thread running through the several chapters is the question of how those moments, demonstrated so far as that is at all possible in the varieties of critical judgment, are themselves possible. The discussion thus moves from an analysis of critical judgment (chapter 2) to the examination in chapter 3 of a precondition of critical judgment (denotation); this serves as a bridge first to a rendering of the aesthetic moment through the medium of the concept of "aesthetic proximity," (chapter 4), and then to an analysis of those objects and contexts by means of which the distinctive appearance of aesthetic objects in general is made intelligible (and possible).

Transcendental argument inevitably faces systematic objections as it presupposes criteria for a conception of possibility: there seem to be innumerable possible categories that can subsume a generic moment of experience (if only because of the alternative descriptions to which that moment is initially open). The basis for deciding among those categories, furthermore, is the more difficult to ascertain, the more comprehensive the categories are supposed to be. This problem is both evident and serious, for example, in Kant's statement of method (specifically in the Transcendental Deduction), even as that statement prefaced the most sustained application yet given that method. It is, I suppose, at once the weakness and strength of my account that I fashion its terms in such a way as to avoid the problem, by representing *its* conception of possibility only as possible, not as necessary. Perhaps that conception is also necessary; indeed, given the description of the aesthetic moment which is cited, I would argue that it is. But I do not see that the same case can be made for the description itself. In any event, the thicket of discussion surrounding the possibility of the "necessity" of a transcendental deduction is so dense that I have thought it useful to commit the argument only to the weaker thesis. The last word on the question of that necessity—and thus indeed on the analysis undertaken here—will in any event not be spoken in a work for which aesthetic inquiry is primary.

The issues thus defined are resilient, but nonetheless tractable. As a guide to the character of The Possible, we have always at hand The Actual and the judgments on which *it* insists. The skeptic will reply that such a claim does no more than make inevitability into a virtue. Perhaps. But without a continual turning to the "datum in the actual world," what is probable or even only possible must be reckoned as still less than that; with the turning, a chance exists for placing the elements of experience in a pattern of conceptual contrast—that is, for comprehending them at all.

A feature of my method is that the line of argument passes through a number of stages which can to some extent be assessed independently. To ask how the judgments of criticism are possible is to leave open the question of how the work of art is possible. To be sure, the latter question makes no sense unless the presuppositions in the former have been granted and unless one of a particular class of answers has been given it. But even such a constrained answer to the first question allows a number of alternative answers for the second; and analogous relations connect the sequence of essays in this volume. Although those essays are intended, then, to form a whole and to hang together, perhaps certain of them must hang separately. Enough will survive, I hope, to suggest a substance for aesthetic inquiry as well as a method.

Acknowledgment by itself is rather less than a fair return for their efforts, if only because of its implication of collective responsibility. But I feel obliged to thank a number of institutions and people who have undertaken, the former to support, the latter to improve, this book. The former include the Rothschild Foundation of the Hebrew University, the Lucius N. Littauer Foundation, the National Endowment for the Humanities, and the Council on Research of the University of Colorado. I am especially indebted to friends who have read and commented on the book—to Albert Hofstadter, Leonard Boonin, Irwin C. Lieb, Paul Levitt, Paul J. W. Miller, Gary Stahl, and Forrest Williams.

Early and abbreviated versions of chapters 1, 3, and 4 appeared in the *Journal of Aesthetics and Art Criticism* 27 (1968), *The British Journal of Aesthetics* 10 (1970), and the *International Philosophical Quarterly* 11 (1971), respectively.

Boulder, Colorado   B.L.
October, 1973

I A Context for Inquiry

"Das Schöne verdankt nicht der Äesthetik sein Dasein."

G. Wolandt

1

The Form
of Aesthetics

Many writers on aesthetics in the recent philosophical literature of Great Britain and the United States have proposed rather to bury it than to praise it. And although one need only point to the work in aesthetics on the European continent and in certain Anglo-American pockets of resistance to find assurance that reports of its death—like those eulogizing Mark Twain while he was alive—are exaggerated, it may be well to consider the morphology of these obituaries. Whether the arguments are mistaken or not, they point a moral for philosophical inquiry: if aesthetics *is* dead, it remains a monument in futility to the work of aestheticians who might have been; if it survives, the realization may serve as a therapeutic to the techniques of philosophical criticism which have contrived to overlook that detail. In either event, we stand to gain a clearer view of a form.

The principal objections to the work of aesthetics have been twofold: first, that in a verbose career it has little to show for the goal assumed by aestheticians of providing definitions of beauty or art; second, that its failure in this respect, given its prior failure to qualify as a philosophical enterprise, has been necessary, not accidental. I shall not be considering the former of these objections. It may be, as Santayana suggests, that aesthetics (at least up to the time when he writes about it in *The Sense of Beauty*) had undergone no rigorous philosophical treatment; and that today it still remains in the "stone-age" of its history to which Arnold Isenberg, one of the most incisive contemporary philosophers of art, consigned it. These assessments seem in fact to underestimate the force exerted in the course of Western philosophy by the issues and conclusions of aesthetic inquiry. Even if one were to grant such estimates of the accomplishments of aesthetics, however, it would not follow, as has sometimes been supposed, that the philosophy of art is impossible as an enterprise. Admittedly, if it were true that the conclusions of aesthetics in the past had failed on every count to illuminate the objects of art, this would be evidence of a problematic base. But few of the critics of aesthetic analysis have ventured this claim; the fact that to do so would question the possibility of actual works by philosophers of the order of Aristotle and Kant has surely and rightly been a factor in that reticence.

The Empirical Ground. It would be an irrelevance, however, to judge the prospect for aesthetics by arguing that the criticism of the claims made for it has been equivocal. A verdict on that criticism must confront its substantive objection, in particular the thesis that "traditional" aesthetics (the critics usually link it to a similar tendency of traditional philosophy in general) has reflected in the a priori determination of its subject matter and method, a dogmatic character which supplies a ready epitaph for its failures. One such statement appears in William Kennick's essay, "Does Traditional Aesthetics Rest on a Mistake?" which I refer to here because of its representative formulation of this criticism.[1] Kennick, answering his own question in the affirmative, isolates two problematic themes of aesthetics: first, the assumption that "all works of art must possess some common nature, some distinctive set of characteristics which serve to separate art from everything else" (p. 319); and second, the assumption that "criticism presupposes aesthetic theory . . . [or] that responsible criticism is impossible without standards or criteria universally applicable to all works of art" (p. 325). In pointing out these "mistakes," Kennick does not explicitly deny the possibility of aesthetics; but it seems unlikely that aesthetics, in his view of its traditional form, could survive the loss of what he regards as its central premises.

I shall consider the second part of this criticism later in this chapter. The first objection is closer to the central question of the viability of aesthetic inquiry. The claim is made in that objection that the writers on aesthetics characteristically strike an arbitrary stance in the very conception of their work, assuming dogmatically that the objects which they assume to be the objects of their inquiry *must* share certain properties, possession of which is then "perceived" as a distinguishing feature. The work of traditional aesthetics has proceeded, the argument goes, from this question-begging basis; the assumption itself being factitious, however, whatever follows from it or answers to it stands similarly condemned. For there are a variety of manners and objects of art; the contention that this variety is dominated by certain common elements or even by a certain group of elements is gratuitous in origin and empirically false.

This criticism includes two separate assertions. One of these is that the writers on aesthetics have affirmed the existence of common and distinctively "aesthetic" features in certain objects or moments of experience; the second is that they have reached this conclusion arbitrarily, in effect by legislating the existence or the quality of "aesthetic" attributes which they then take to constitute the subject of aesthetic inquiry. These two assertions are of quite different degrees of interest, the first being only of slight interest despite its truth. Even if we object to the vagaries of the phrase "traditional" aesthetics (there are, after all, a multitude of traditional sinners to choose from; do we mean the work of Plato? Aquinas? Hume?), the first claim seems generally accurate. In much, if not all, of what we would ordinarily regard as writings in the philosophy of art, a thesis recurs according to which characteristic properties belong to "aesthetic" objects or situations; thus, for example, the common function of terms like "harmony," "unity in complexity," "expression," or "beauty." It is clear from the contexts in which such references appear, furthermore, that the properties they designate have sometimes been regarded as distinguishing certain objects or situations from others which are then held to be nonaesthetic or at least less aesthetic.

This practice by itself, however, is hardly exceptionable; what is claimed verges on tautology, asserting no more than that objects and situations in general stand at various distances from those of aesthetic quality, that aesthetic "things" differ from nonaesthetic "things," or—to make the tautology quite explicit—that the objects of aesthetic inquiry are the objects of aesthetic inquiry. The drive behind the practice is reflected even in the statement by which Kennick objects to it. Thus, he argues against the assumption that works of art share certain properties: "All we see [in observing works of art] is this poem and that play, this picture and that statue . . . and if we find some resemblances between poems or plays or pictures, or even between poems and pictures, pictures and musical compositions, those resemblances quickly disappear when we turn to other poems and plays and pictures" (p. 319). Kennick then criticizes the blindness of the tradition to this point; but in formulating his objection, he does not hesitate to assume the admissibility of the concept of the class of "works of art" by means of which poems and plays and pictures are selected out. Thus he implies that the features which define that concept can be recognized; we are expected to understand that the phrase designates a group of objects identifiable by some criteria, even if they are unspoken;[2] Kennick's criticism, then, itself claims as much as what it objects to in the practice of aestheticians who explicitly identify certain objects or moments of "art" by that class or generic name.

The second part of the criticism cited is thus the more pressing of the two. The objection here is not that the writers of aesthetics have circumscribed certain objects or moments of experience but that in doing so they have ignored the philosophical proprieties. The assumption made concerning the common features of aesthetic objects is gratuitous, betraying either indifference or carelessness in the face of the evidence. Such features, quite simply, do not exist. The assertions to the contrary have at best the defect of faulty empirical generalization; at worst, the ring of a priori reasoning about matters of fact.

What is important about this part of the objection is that it insists upon indicting aesthetics—at least one common conception of aesthetics—on systematic grounds which are more fundamental than any accusation of historical "failure." It is directed not only at the apologiae given for aesthetics by its past advocates, but at those which might be given for any future or possible aesthetics in which the concept appears of art as such. Even if the writer on aesthetics were willing to assume more than a priori responsibility for the premises from which he traditionally operated, his design must fail: neither experience nor pure reason will support it.

This argument turns against an important version of the enterprise of aesthetics, and a reply to it must be no less comprehensive in its claims. I shall argue both that the contested basis of traditional aesthetics need not be gratuitous and that writers even in the heterodox past of aesthetics have in general been aware of the importance that it should not be. If devisors of actual systems of aesthetics have circumvented that large objection, there can be little doubt of the formal possibility that this may be so. This fact suggests a systematic principle that may underwrite the work of aesthetics: that the process of aesthetic inquiry, past or future, has access to an empirical ground for its characteristic assertion of the common features of aesthetic objects.

Such a claim can hardly be argued here with respect to the work of each of the major figures in the past; nor do I attempt in this context to provide a specific representation of that claim as it *ought* to be formulated. (This can emerge only in the actual work of aesthetic inquiry.) A foundation can be discriminated however, which will by analogy apply to many, if not all, of the larger figures in traditional aesthetics. Consider, for example, the systematic basis to the aesthetic theory of so casual a methodologist as Croce. In the first chapter of his *Guide to Aesthetics*,[3] Croce approaches the question of What is art? by viewing and rejecting a number of possible answers. He distinguishes between art, on the one hand (he applies the term to both the "process" and the "product"), and "physical fact," "conceptual knowledge," and "utilitarian moral acts," on the other. In assessing the relation between each of these and the work or process of art,

21

Croce explicitly tests the empirical consequences if art were equated with them. If, for example, the art object were no more than another physical object, the interest shown in a piece of sculpture by an art critic and by a man hired to move it should have the same character. But, to enlarge on the example, it is clear that when the mover says that he is troubled by the dimensions of the sculpture, he is responding to different aspects of the work from those considered by the critic who makes the same statement. And we know this difference from our own direct experience of those processes: the dimensions cited in the two judgments are "visibly" different, as a matter of function if not quite of fact. Again, in considering the relation of art to moral action, Croce argues that we tend to assess the goodness of a moral agent by judging the character of his will or intentions. Our evaluation of an artist, however, is quite different; we judge *him* by his works. And we know this difference not by legislating definitions or by exercising a privileged intuition of aesthetic and moral value, but by examining the empirical ground which underlies the conventional distinctions between moral and aesthetic judgment.

The issue here is not whether Croce is convincing in his analysis of physical object or of moral action or of art itself. What is pertinent is that, in rejecting several possible accounts of art, Croce takes responsibility for measuring them by the experience purportedly connected to art; and that the accounts he rejects, he at least claims to reject in terms of that experience. His conclusions circumscribe a variety of experience distinguishable from certain other varieties; the latter simply do not represent art as we encounter it.

It could be shown, I think, that most of the important writers in the history of aesthetics have carried on their work with a similarly empirical methodological premise explicitly before them. To be sure, if the objection to the procedures of aesthetics is psychological in force—that is, if it is an objection to an inclination or prejudice of certain writers to assert that there must be beautiful objects and/or to see beauty as the single common attribute of such objects—there is no answering it. But neither, given the problematic status of psychological explanation (and of *ad hominem* argument), can much be said in its defense. All that we have to go on is what is said in the writings on aesthetics. And in those writings, including even the work of a supposed arch-advocate of "revisionary metaphysics" like Plato, it is clear that the impulse behind the analysis of such aesthetic qualities as beauty is not that beauty must exist, but that, in the sense in which "things" ever are said to be, there is such a thing to which experience itself testifies. Perhaps these writers identify the character of the aesthetic moment only after they have begun to look for it; but this is far from implying that the existence of that character or moment begins even in their own minds only with the looking.

Admittedly, aesthetic theories have on occasion gone beyond the range of the data from which they set out. This is a plausible objection to Croce's expansion of the concept of expression in his own system. But one can hardly ascribe responsibility for later abuses of a principle to an earlier and more limited intention. Or again, the possibility exists that the supposedly common points of origin of various aesthetic systems, notwithstanding their empirical focus, still differ substantively at the point of focus or in the logic of abstraction which follows it.[4] We may mistake verbal differences and agreements in the initial descriptions for real differences or agreements among aesthetic theories. This danger, however, is not peculiar to aesthetics. Any simple appeal to empirical referents may appear to agree or disagree with another appeal when it really does not: the risk, it seems, is endemic to discourse itself.

If I seem to labor the formal claim for the possibility of the empirical basis of aesthetics, the reason is that little can be said by way of argument which would establish that actual basis. One cannot, to state the obvious, demonstrate the objects (or fact) of experience; and the premise in aesthetic theory that (a) distinctive moment(s) of experience can be discerned which constitute(s) the subject matter of the theory thus remains undemonstrated. But the fact that aesthetic inquiry lacks a deductive foundation does not mean that its conceptual claims will not be sound or flawed in the same way as are any statements which purportedly derive from and reflect on the world of matter-of-fact.

These comments on the genealogy of aesthetics do not imply assent to a particular system. Neither do they define the method which any such system ought to employ, or argue the importance of the enterprise itself. *Why* we do (or should) attempt philosophical understanding of certain junctures of experience, and what methods or categories can (or should) be applied in the analysis are questions still to be considered. These questions suggest a purpose for this discussion larger than that of showing only that on empirical grounds the work of aesthetics is possible. And to be sure, I hope both to claim a role for aesthetics in the philosophical enterprise and to characterize that role. The prospect for either of the latter moves would be doomed beforehand, however, if the limited point made in this section were not taken: that systems of aesthetics are potentially (if only because in general they have been in fact) bound by an empirical protocol. When Kant (to cite what seems to me a conclusive example) analyzes the judgment of taste, suspicion may well be roused by the way in which his conclusions about that judgment complement his prior analysis of pure and practical reason, by the systematic neatness with which the conceptions of beauty and the sublime in the Third Critique cap the building stones set down in the faculty and categorial distinctions of the *Critique of Pure Reason* and the *Critique of Practical Reason*. But this suspicion by itself fails to acknowledge the basic premise to which Kant commits himself in the *Critique of Aesthetic Judgment* and without which he could hardly be held to account for anything else he claims there; namely, that there *are* judgments of taste and that they characteristically differ from cognitive and moral judgments. This premise is not a priori or merely stipulative; thus, viewed from the standpoint neither of its function nor of its purpose can it be called arbitrary, as the criticism considered here would have it. Mistaken, perhaps, or otiose, but not arbitrary or dogmatic.

Aesthetics and the Process of Philosophical Inquiry. To defend the empirical charter of aesthetics is not yet to substantiate its philosophical claims. In this connection we have to go beyond the question of the possibility of aesthetics to that of its possible value. The latter issue is not easily handled; for if we approach it with the conviction that aesthetics is part of the enterprise of philosophy, then to study its function is to raise the question of what the design of philosophy is. There is no way of avoiding or ignoring that connection; and in developing the hint that aesthetic inquiry begins with a version of the same wonder in which Plato suggests that philosophy as a whole originates, we face at both levels the question left over by that genealogy as to the object of the "wonder": what it is at or about, and what the form of its resolution may be.

One classical response to this question designates what I shall refer to as the explanatory role of philosophy, and I shall argue that a plausible conception of aesthetics can be formulated in terms of this role. To be sure, one knows of denials that there is anything which answers to the name of philosophical explanation; we hear frequently that the task of philosophy is to explicate criteria or to determine rules of linguistic usage, but specifically not to explain or to describe. We do not need to fight this battle here except to enter a single qualification: no reason is evident for assuming that these putative functions of philosophy are incompatible. I shall be explicating, then, what I take to be an important but not necessarily exhaustive function of philosophy and of aesthetics. Advocates of certain views of philosophy may not wish their accounts reconciled with the notion of philosophical explanation outlined below; but this, too, must give way before the test of the issue itself.

The dependence of aesthetics on the character of philosophical explanation is complicated not only by disputes as to what that character is but by disagreement on the nature of explanation in itself and quite aside from philosophy. Provisionally, I refer to the generic aspects of this question—the *ambitions* of explanation—through the Aristotelian concept of the *aitiae*, the "causes" in terms of which Aristotle identifies the form of explanation. This is not to imply that those causes or principles are equally relevant to every instance of explanation or that the distinctions among them are impermeable (witness the attempts to reduce the final cause to a combination of material and efficient causes).[5] But Aristotle suggests that together the *aitiae* exhaust the forms of explanation developed prior to his analysis; they are, first if not finally, the discoveries of practice, of what explanation had aspired to be.[6] Philosophical progress since the time of Aristotle's outline has not, I contend, substantially controverted his functional delineation of explanation.

This schema, however, does not provide a conceptual definition of what explanation is or show how any particular explanation may be distinguished as "philosophical." With respect to the former issue: disputes have proliferated in recent epistemology on the character of explanation. What emerges from those discussions is not very different from and perhaps even less precise than the classical conceptions of a process which advances from "the more familiar to the more intelligible." The "covering law" model, the most immediately plausible of the accounts recently current, holds that the crucial feature of an explanation is its articulation of a general principle under which what is to be explained is subsumable;[7] thus, that the test of the principle is whether the phenomenon can be grasped in terms of it, perhaps causally or as a prediction, but at any rate, as comprehended or understood. To know, for example, Darwin's principle of natural selection is to understand (so far as the principle holds) the formal pattern of the particular characteristics of animal species. Various inadequacies have been attributed to this model; without denying their force, I shall be adducing it here. At the least, and for all of the objections to that model, it may serve to revive the important formal connection between philosophical and scientific explanation.

The problems in deriving a conception of explanation in general are broader but no deeper than the difficulties in identifying the concept of philosophical explanation: we still have to ask, if we agree about the general form of explanation, what distinguishes its "philosophical" appearance. The latter question is pointed sharply if we substitute for "philosophical" any of several other predicates, for example, "psychological," "economic," "physiological." We do not expect a psychological explanation to end with a description of fluctuations in the stock market. Even if it reflects only a provisional distinction among types of objects, we assume that psychological explanation draws its parameters from mental events and not from variations in the supply of gold. But no such circumscribed set of objects appears at the locus of philosophical explanation. Prima facie, an account which concludes with a description of the fluctuations of the stock market would not count as philosophical explanation. Furthermore, as we look for such a reference, a persistent lack becomes evident: there seems to be no specific subject matter, no circumscribed group of events or objects comparable to those governing the work of economics or psychology, which sets even an approximate limit for the philosophical idiom.

To acknowledge this is to hint at a role for philosophy implicit in the sense of wonder which Socrates commended to Theaetetus; that is, that philosophy is an attempt to understand what there is in the most radical sense of "is"—and thus, also, according to standards or categories of a corresponding degree of generality. In Aristotle's terms, this object of philosophical understanding is represented as being *qua* being. The force, even the sense, of this conception has been questioned, but a number of formal considerations support it. It accounts for the difficulty of assigning to philosophy a subject matter analogous to that ascribed in the examples of economics or psychology cited above: philosophy would not have one. It furthermore anticipates the forms of inquiry ordinarily accepted as philosophical. The concern of the philosopher of science, for example, is not to establish particular uniformities or laws but to identify the more general epistemic status of such laws; the work of the moral philosopher is not to formulate particular items of social legislation but the principles from which such legislation obtains. The emphasis in such proceedings is not on the imposition of restrictive categories on data of a proportionately limited kind but in the most general understanding of the data possible.

It is admittedly difficult to enumerate the general questions which comprise such an investigation; it is difficult even to indicate how they might be identified. It is unclear, finally, what shape the answers to such questions will assume. The force of these problems can be mitigated, however, by a process of exclusion or negative proof. Consider first certain alternatives to the study of "being as being." One alternative is an analysis confined to a single aspect of experience, proceeding by means of categories which are themselves restricted by some special pertinence. The physiologist, for example, studies the organic systems and functions of living beings; he does not consider whatever is extra- or sub-organic about them, or the careers of nonorganic objects. He scrutinizes such systems, furthermore, not by way of general categories—in other words, not as objects *simpliciter*—but in terms of their physical existence and processes, and thus by specific criteria of analysis and verification that respond specifically to that condition. As a discipline, then—as what I call a first-order science—the object of physiology is a restricted mode of experience; the means for its work, furthermore, are provided by a correspondingly restricted set of critical instruments or principles.

A contrast thus begins to emerge between such analysis and the work of philosophy. The objects on which the philosopher (here I refer especially to the metaphysician) focuses are not organic entities in particular but the class of entities of which organic entities are a subclass. He seeks for that general class, furthermore, not a perspectival account, governed by limited categories directed to a particular one of its aspects, but an account supported by categories that apply as generally as categories can: not the standards of analysis or verification employed, for example, by physiology, but the standards from which those standards derive. (The two orders of analysis, it should be noted, are not incompatible; where this proves the case, it reflects internal error in one or the other or both of the orders. What is true of being in general will be true if not a fortiori, at least a priori, of its species.)

A number of questions persist concerning the character of

the objects scrutinized by the metaphysician and the status of the categories applicable to them. It is useful to approach such questions by way of a more specific one about the relation between aesthetics, on the one hand, and the first-order sciences and metaphysics, on the other. For it becomes evident from the map on which these other enterprises have been located that the position left on that map for aesthetics straddles the line between the orders of analysis disclosed in the principal distinction so far noted. Aesthetic inquiry focuses not on all objects or moments but rather on those which, as aesthetic, command a specific and limited attention. If those moments are distinctive, that is, if aesthetics indeed has a circumscribed empirical ground, it then lacks the generality which purportedly is a feature of metaphysics. On the other hand, if aesthetics is not one of the first-order sciences, it will differ in the methodology of its analysis as well. This requirement would be met if the work of aesthetics were not bound to categorial principles determined by conventional stipulation but looked rather to the categories yielded by the general reflection of metaphysics. The writer on aesthetics thus hopes to realize an account of certain moments not in terms of the restricted standards such as those referred by physiology to the varieties of physical shape or process, but "as such." He hopes to identify a certain strain of experience in terms of principles which apply to experience as a whole. It is precisely a question for the writer on aesthetics whether the moments on which he touches are usefully analyzed in terms, for example, of their physiological effects; if it turned out that they were, we could know this only as a consequence of having first looked at the data through more general categories.[8] The work of aesthetics, in other words, will be to consider *aesthetic* being *qua* being, and not *qua* any of the subspecies by which the first-order sciences are bound; it holds an intermediate place in a formal structure which extends from the first-order sciences at one limit to metaphysics at the other.

· The assignment of this hybrid character to aesthetics hints at its relations with the enterprises on its borders. On the one hand, aesthetics depends on the first-order sciences as a source of concrete, empirical data—that is, for the data which set the occasion of its questions, attesting to both the existence and qualities of its objects. The initial stimulus to understanding may not have the order or breadth of those sciences, but the difference is one of degree, not of quality. Thus, it is important for aesthetics—at least it is important until the conclusions of aesthetics itself show that it is not—that aestheticians consider the physiological effects of aesthetic experience, just as it is important, initially at least, that writers on aesthetics know the historian's conclusions that styles in the development of art are (or are not) functions of economic modes of production. It is only by the light of such sources that the first discrimination of a class of moments is even possible.

On the other hand, the work of aesthetics will in part be dependent on metaphysics for the categories or principles by means of which it comprehends the data registered in the first-order sciences. If aesthetic inquiry is concerned with accounting for the distinctive features of aesthetic objects—in effect, then, like the philosophy of science or political philosophy, a second-order science—it requires for the task an overarching concept of what objects are, of the general categories in terms of which any particular species of object can be located, and thus through which the distinguishing features of aesthetic objects can be articulated. There is little point in asking about the peculiarities of temporal process in the aesthetic moment unless that discussion is juxtaposed to an account of process aside from that experience; there would be small profit, if it were possible at all, in analyzing the referential force of art without placing it against a broader concept of reference. Given the limited character of the first-order sciences, it is from a source in another and larger order that such general categories may come.

I do not mean that in this topography the lines of division among the orders of inquiry are either sharp or impermeable, or even that they are strictly hierarchical (in this respect, the use of terms like "first-order" and "second-order" may be misleading). Nor do I imply that the commerce between aesthetics and its concrete sources is unidirectional or that the sources themselves are autonomous. The specific ways in which those sources are reciprocally related to aesthetics will be discussed at a later point; but it may be apparent even now that the orders of inquiry between which aesthetics would on this account be functioning are refractory. The projects of the first-order sciences primarily involve the collection and analysis of concrete data. But as the standard criticism of those sciences has made increasingly clear, the concrete data assimilated in them do not by themselves yield the principles applied in their selection and processing. Such principles draw for their structure and direction on the overarching principles ascribed first to the conclusions of metaphysics, and, at a lesser level of abstraction, to the intermediate disciplines, like aesthetics. Metaphysics itself, in contrast, as has been consistently clear in its central traditions, depends for its stimulus and for the quality of its organization and limits on the common world of discourse and experience; it thus depends on the first-order sciences as they make that world apparent.

The form of aesthetics will be, then, functionally distinct from the forms of other orders of analysis. So far as method alone is concerned, however, the procedures of the various orders show strong similarities; it is with this in mind that the generic features of the work of aesthetics were referred to Aristotle's "causes." From an initial (pre-reflective) awareness of aesthetic "moments," the writer on aesthetics is then faced with examining their varieties and power: the "stuff" and limits of the experience—what, on the one hand, constitutes the raw material from which the aesthetic "moment" unfolds and on the other hand, what (given the experience) shapes and distinguishes it as a moment of experience (the material and formal causes); the impulses of human nature and the stimuli in the world which act to set the process in motion (the efficient cause); and what the aesthetic experience aims at, its consequences and significance for those who encounter it and for the universe of discourse of which both they and the experience are part (the final cause).

These questions both delimit aesthetic inquiry and justify it; they are warranted by the form of inquiry itself, as inquiry has been practiced. The account in which this is accepted as a basis

31

will be verified or disproved, at any rate, in the discussions which presuppose it. As I conceive of them, these questions imply the requirements of the "covering-law model." A larger question of which the different "causes" themselves are aspects is simply, why the given—aesthetic—moment is as it is. The answers provided by the different causes will have the form of general, law-like statements in terms of which the particular instance of the aesthetic object or experience follows or becomes intelligible.[9] To know, for example, the constitutive elements of aesthetic objects and the impulses ascribed to their potential viewers (the efficient cause) would be at least so far to "understand" the origin of any particular response of a viewer to art, certainly in retrospect and perhaps (although this is more complicated) in prospect.[10] To have a conception of the material cause of art in general would provide an understanding of the aesthetic difference which different media make, for instance, for marking the difference in aesthetic potentiality between a sonata and a painting.

I have avoided thus far the issue of whether there is an aesthetic subject matter on which the formal apparatus outlined above may act. That issue, obviously, is never far removed from the present discussion. The questions of "how aesthetic experience is possible" and "how to account for the aesthetic object," which I take to be summary evocations of the form of aesthetics, are complex questions which themselves assume a subject matter. Even to inquire after the nature of art of aesthetic experience is to impose conditions on the answer. An account of the source, even if that source never appears explicitly, is implied throughout the work of aesthetic inquiry; logically, it stands at the center of any aesthetic system. But it is no more the task of the writer on aesthetics to exhibit that center than it is for him to be judged on the merits of his paintings or poems. Aesthetics would not be possible without the "fact" of art; but the aesthetician can only hope to end with a representation of the fact, not of art itself. The practice of aesthetics necessarily precedes the definition, let alone the re-creation of its source. Indeed, its work is a constant reaching back, a pulling on its own bootstraps. If aesthetic inquiry is successful even in its own terms, it will provide understanding, not new art.[11] The most that we can expect from aesthetic inquiry, then, is testimony to a source and reflection on it. In chapter 2, I shall show just where that testimony begins and the direction toward which it points. But this is a project separate from the present one. The questions raised thus far concern the form of "any possible aesthetics." The assertions of any actual aesthetics, I have been arguing, can be required (and expected) to stand on their own.

Aesthetics and Criticism. The form of aesthetics and its relations with the orders of inquiry around it is further illuminated by consideration of the second objection to traditional aesthetics—the alleged proprietary attitude of its practitioners toward criticism, and specifically their assumption that critical criteria and their application depend on the conclusions of aesthetic theory. As was true for the first objection against the supposedly a priori character of traditional aesthetics, this one too argues against a feature ascribed both historically and systematically to the structure of aesthetics. More than the other objection, however, this one is historically misleading. In numerous important moments in the history of aesthetics, most notably in the related work of eighteenth-century British empiricism and Kant, a strong case has been made for the subjective, nontheoretical character of critical judgment, particularly in its evaluative appearances. There is, then, nothing even superficially novel about such a challenge. Nevertheless, attempts have been made to establish sets of necessary and sufficient conditions for critical judgment, in the form of "essential" properties such as unity or harmony or clarity; and the task of defining these conditions has often been assigned to aesthetics. An estimate of what underlies such attempts requires a more comprehensive study of the history of criticism than will be undertaken here; but in anticipation of such a study, I would offer a number of comments about the claims of "rationalistic" aesthetics.

One matter in this connection seems especially pertinent: that whatever the ostensive conception of the function or logic of criticism is, critical judgment, as a matter of *fact*, is often linked to the work of aesthetics. To cite one obvious connection: the art critic can hardly avoid speaking of the work of art. Either that term in itself or in one or several of its elements (the meter of a poem or the hands of a painted figure) is the subject of every critical investigation, perhaps of every sentence of critical discourse. But the histories of both criticism and aesthetics amply testify that the denotation of such terms, far from being self-evident, is often a subject of dispute. What does the critic assert when, for example, he writes of the "beauty" of Cellini's *Perseus*? Is he designating a primary quality of the piece of bronze behind which children play hide-and-go-seek in the Piazza della Signoria? Is he judging an illusion projected by that object to an "ideal spectator"? Or the formal lines of either of those objects? The emotion of the artist as he created it, or the moral response of the observer? Each (and any combination) of these meanings—and they are not exhaustive—has been ascribed to the judgment. The critic's choice among them determines both what any particular judgment amounts to and more generally what, as critic, he sets himself to judge.

It follows from such alternatives that ostensively identical or consistent critical judgments may represent quite different, even contradictory responses. It thus also follows that until the decisions required by these questions for both the critic and his reader have been settled, neither can take much comfort from statements of apparent critical agreement. The critic may sometimes be at a loss for judgment, not through any fault in taste, but because of a prior failure to answer certain conceptual questions on the form of aesthetics. The need for sorting out such general issues both separates aesthetics from criticism and establishes a connection between them. The fact that critics and readers of criticism are often uncritical in their handling of the question of what principles underlie their judgments and that writers on aesthetics do not always take pains to see how their principles end in experience is a comment rather on practice than on the challenge of the issues themselves.

The dependence of criticism on aesthetics is related to the

structural framework of criticism, not to the characteristically individual decisions we expect of critics. But as it turns out, these two aspects of the critical process are not easily separated. When a critic appraises an art object, in one clear sense he is not carrying on the work of aesthetics; yet in another sense, no less clear (unless to begin with we assume a radically subjective theory of criticism that limits critical judgment to feeling alone, and feeling itself to a series of simple and discrete moments) his judgment is supported by concepts and by criteria related to them. Elements of these concepts and criteria extend beyond what is given in any particular occasion of criticism. On even the most rationalistic account of critical judgment, a contingent and to this extent autonomous response is involved, if only as the assertion is made that certain critical criteria are or are not met in the judgment. Thus, to hold that necessary and sufficient conditions, such as unity or coherence, can establish or disprove the aesthetic significance of a given object is not in itself to deny the singularity and contingency of the context in which critical judgment is passed. From the other side, there is also no reason to assume that the application of critical instruments and the quality of appreciation itself are closed to history and its emendations, that conceptual analysis plays no role in that application. In fact, the prima facie evidence concerning the development of taste testifies to the contrary; even the availability of aesthetic quality as an option of experience may be determined by such reflection for viewers of art who do not find it spontaneously. The claim that radically sensuous experience (which is probably *not* what aesthetic experience is) is closed to expansion or contraction by way of conceptual analysis suggests an "emotional a priori" liable to objections similar to those raised against most, if not all, formulations of the a priori categories of understanding: the categories are not, strictly speaking, a priori.

This, again, does not mean that conceptual analysis is either a vehicle or a substitute for the concrete response to art; I suggest only that any such response is not "absolutely" concrete, and that among the abstractions which figure in it are reflections on aesthetic issues. It is not that aesthetics is logically or axiologically prior to criticism, but only that criticism, as practice reveals it, is systematically linked to aesthetics. The relation of the two recalls the Aristotelian distinction between theoretical and practical science, a distinction located principally in the apparent ends of those disciplines which may be identified in the differences between understanding and doing. The work of aesthetics, I have suggested, is an attempt to explain, to provide understanding of, an aspect of experience. Avoiding elaboration for the moment, I construe the proximate end of criticism as the practical education of taste, the effecting in the viewer of a realization of particular objects, the providing of techniques and patterns of sensing for carrying on the performance of the spectator. The findings of the aesthetician take the form of general principles. This concern is with the characteristic aesthetic moment and the work of art as such; the fact that his data are particulars noted in experience serves only as a preface to his hope of discerning some general order among them. Criticism, on the other hand, focuses on the particular work of art which aesthetics goes beyond. Even critical generalizations concerning a period or style both begin and end in judgments about particular objects. Criticism, like any practical science, comes finally to a point where individual decision and action rule; but it does not begin or end there. The attentiveness and sensitivity of taste are emergent and educable; taste at any moment in its history both depends on and represents, both in its virtues and faults, a conceptual substructure which it is also the business of aesthetics, not of criticism alone, to act on. If we think of aesthetics as a version of applied metaphysics, criticism, which proceeds further in the same direction, becomes applied aesthetics. Theoretical understanding, though it may not move practical action, articulates it when it does move. To judge an object as beautiful may not be to speculate or to make decisions or even consciously to discriminate; but the logical connections between that judgment and its ground assure the phantom presence of all of these activities.

For the purposes of argument, the emphasis here has been on the implications of aesthetics for criticism; but aesthetics is in turn dependent on the practice of criticism. Its explanatory principles could only miss the point to which they aspire were it not for the activity of criticism as it sharpens perception and appreciation and, finally, as it marks the occasion from which aesthetics sets out; the conclusions of criticism serve as evidence by which the explanations offered by aesthetics are tested. The principles asserted by aesthetics are contingent on findings and data which represent the contingencies of experience. This process concludes in what must be a commonplace to readers of the history of aesthetics, namely, that aesthetic systems (no less than critical systems and judgments) are dialectical both in their individual development and in the historical pattern of which they are all part. They change as the inclusive metaphysical context varies; they are also responsive to the urgencies of the concrete moment. Even in a Platonic world, after all, the recognition of Beauty—whatever the constancy of Beauty itself—takes time.

Conceptual Verification and the Logic of Aesthetics. The dialectical pattern that marks the development of aesthetic theories also defines the problems involved in their evaluation. The most obvious of these difficulties is that there will be no historical point at which the questions posed by aesthetics are settled: the evidence, however circumspectly it is accumulated, will never be all in. As Hegel suggests, the very concept of art (and no less art itself) may at some point be obsolete; their very existence, and not only their respective forms, is historical and contingent. A fortiori, so long as it lives, art (and the projects that reflect on it) is open to the same attenuation and expansion to which its past history has been a constant witness.

Such intrinsic incompleteness does not, however, imply that the assessment of aesthetic theories is impossible. They are at least as open to criticism as the philosophical systems of which they are part; and both the problems and possibilities of evaluating them appear in this fact. If, to take the difficulties first, we acknowledge it as a function of philosophy to give an account which is as general as possible, then it seems that any such account must provide its own criteria of adequacy (since there could be no other source). I should argue that such principles of adequacy are implied a priori in the concept of explanation that has already been adduced here—specifically, the Principle of Applicability and the Principle of Coherence. The former of these criteria requires that an explanation "apply" to the material which it purports to explain, both as to its elements and to the whole. This implies the use of a subordinate criterion of relevance: the elements which compose the material must, after all, pertain to each other in such a manner that an explanation is both possible and apposite. The Principle of Coherence requires that an explanation, formally and independently of any particular application as well as in it, should be logically consistent or "tight"; this represents in effect a formal demand for consistency.[12]

To claim a priori status for these principles may seem to beg an important question. But if it is true that they are implied in the concept of explanation, then the attempt to ground or to explain them is necessarily and not arbitrarily foreclosed; if they are not so implied, this will become apparent, insofar as it ever can, as their applications reveal discrepancies which they cannot govern. Their appearances within aesthetic theory, in other words, will provide whatever justification is possible for the criteria themselves. Such principles, to the extent that they measure aesthetic theory, also (sometimes at the same time) test the professions of philosophical systems in general; and although it may be difficult on occasion, at either level, to see how the principles apply, other occasions make this disposition quite explicit. Thus, it may seem—I do not say that it *is*—fruitless to assess the philosophical systems or even the aesthetic theories of Aristotle and Kant as wholes; but it is certainly meaningful (and, I would argue, justifiable) to criticize the formalist thesis of Roger Fry in terms of the principle of applicability, on the grounds that it fails to take adequate account of the aesthetic "facts" of literature; or to cite Dewey's conception of the art object for its failure to reach beyond the concrete experience of art to its ontological conditions. Again, with respect to the principle of coherence, it can be argued that Kant's juxtaposition in the theory of aesthetic judgment of the ideal of "free beauty" and of his version of Aesthetic Ideas does not hold together consistently. At any rate, the principles governing such objections provide standards of evaluation by which the discussion in the chapters after this may be measured.

To touch on the question of evaluation in an analysis of method is unavoidably to call attention to the issue of the status of that analysis—a perplexing question for the foregoing discussion. Construing in prospect as well as in retrospect the formal structure of aesthetics, such analysis is hardly integral to the substantive work of aesthetics; it is evidently not integral to it in the same sense as would be the questions which touch, for example, on the origin of art. Nor does it deal directly with questions of either metaphysics or criticism, despite the suggestions about their location and their implications for (and from) aesthetics. The work of such analysis attempts rather to outline the relationships among these various enterprises, to indicate the projects and method which they define *for* aesthetics.

The discussion thus comes closest, I suggest, to a statement about the logic of aesthetics—a description of a form, even if it is only of the form that aesthetics would have if an aesthetic subject matter, so far assumed to exist for the sake of form's argument, had been identified. Philosophical fashion notwithstanding, there remain good grounds for viewing logic in its traditional role of organon, providing a purchase on the relations among the elements in a context, determining what can be done to them or with them. The elements and thus the formal pattern will vary from context to context; it is one such grasp of context, based on the elements that are proposed to apply in aesthetics, that has been represented here. I hope in the other essays to show how the actual practice of aesthetics unfolds in the terms of that pattern: how the form can be set to work.

The process of any actual aesthetics, according to this account, reflects a more extensive underlying conception of philosophy; its status can be no more sound or more productive than is that conception, with its overarching and general principles of explanation from which those invoked by aesthetics are derivative. This test is independent of the present context. For however it is judged to be met in what has been (or will be) said, the thesis itself remains—that the form of aesthetic inquiry says something, and in the end a good deal, about the general philosophical inquiry of which it is an aspect. The strengths and defects of aesthetics, certainly of any particular one of its formulations, will thus be neither gratuitous nor without a moral.

A last word on the present discussion: my intention has not been only to establish the possibility of aesthetics, and I have not scrupled, in describing what aesthetics ought to do *if* it exists, to intimate also that it *ought* to exist. To be sure, the justification for the latter claim—so far as there is any—will be evident only in the doing. If the formal project outlined is open to criticism, the final test, form and substance inevitably converging, will confront the practice of aesthetics itself. There is a variety of kinds of conclusion which even that test may yield. Looking back from it, we might determine that it is not really the aesthetics of the "tradition" which has been reconstructed here. Or, trying to be as subtle as possible, we might conclude that it is not aesthetics at all that this essay has depicted but another project of the same name. Let the occasion serve, in any event, to move reflection back to the philosophical ground, which makes pertinent either what has been said about aesthetics or these prospective objections—but at least one or the other.

If this final exhortation hardly counts as an item either of logical analysis or of aesthetics, it is not yet arbitrary or a symptom of metaphysical sleight-of-hand. It remains rather as an implication of the initial and independent premise which fortifies the work of philosophy—affirming, to begin with, the importance of understanding what there is before us. Aesthetics, its conclusions will show if it survives at all, is a part of that work.

The Work in Process

To start from the beginning is a simpler aspiration for piety than for invention. Where, after all, do we first know the existence of art? By standing in front of it? Surely it is there that sensibility is first evoked. But to depend on a single moment for theoretical understanding asks of sensibility a power beyond it. At most the individual response speaks with a voice which has echoes; at its least, it adds a biographical record in a world surfeited with histories. There is a project, however, that renders for the individual response more corporate uses, organizing the activities of practice. Even the discovery of such patterns of response will fall short of presenting what the response is a response to. What we remark in it first is only the location of an event; later, if the questions are put aptly, we may know what the event portends, although still, surely, not the event itself.

The temptation, in inquiring after the nature of art, is to say that we must look at man as he lives with it and after it. And (if these were not enough) also as he lives without it. But the solution would then be denser than the question. Somehow, for all the dangers of begging that question, the method must be narrowed. So we look to patterns of experience which run through the encounter, and finally, to one: the talk about and around art. The search is for form in the expression of that discourse, to locate in the process of language the categories that line it–as they might be detected, for example (but less precisely), in the iconic patterns of alphabets or from styles in the customs of applause. Language, as instrument, contrives more than does a hand—as much perhaps as the hand which has a hand. Its structure, *whatever its origin or quality, is continually taking (and giving) shape; among public monuments, none marks and represents encounters so permanently or so discriminately rehearses their texts.*

The dangers in this identification of a method are twofold: that in the process we may exclude other, contrary evidence. (Perhaps what language purports to reveal about art, it exhibits as language and not because art is art.) Or perhaps in thinking that we arrive at art through the language of criticism, we merely conjure up the art to which we "find" the way. In either of these cases, art is a more genuine fiction than fiction consciously devised. Such possibilities have no resolution. The works of criticism represent themselves as criticism of art. If they turn out not to represent art at all, our only hope for gain still comes from following their deceptions to an end.

What, in the echo of such cautionary notes, may we otherwise hope to learn from criticism? One thing at least, from language as symptom: a charter for its source. Thus, a Working Premise: if art did not exist, talk about it would not have been invented. Unless, again, criticism itself is all there is to the inventions of art. But if that were true, there would be little else about which we have not also been misled. The Working Premise thus poses in behalf of language no more than an argument from design. But the opening is important. For if there is reason in the purposes of critical discourse, there will be reason in its forms—with that reason in turn leading beyond (or below) criticism, uncovering the quality of a ground. We cannot know beforehand what (or how much) will appear at the source, more than we might have known (before that) that criticism itself would exist: criticism—its critics insistently remind us—is accidental. So far as its contingencies are not arbitrarily set, however, it may yet tell us more than its makers (or critics) had dreamt.

The resolve thus turns to the primary medium of response—language. That tactic may appear to solicit in behalf of a tyranny which already weighs heavily, in the diminution of philosophy for which symbols appear as middle and end (as well as beginning). The insistence, then, also on a Regulative Principle—

that the language of criticism shall be met as phenomenon, not as norm (even of language, let alone of art). The appearances of criticism, in other words, as function rather than substance. No doubt, criticism claims its own courts and appeals, recourse to unimpeachable justice if not to mercy. But the language of criticism is not pristine either at its end or beginning. The grist ground by its mill comes from all the directions in which sense and innovation extend–surely, for an important possibility, from art itself. To represent language otherwise, like Narcissus, fixed on itself, is to make overtures to a new Platonism which can only leave the old one blushing.

In such consideration, the possibility recurs that art is impervious to criticism, that criticism, having lived by the grace of illusions, will vanish with their dispersion. (How many mourners, one wonders, would be in the crowd at that funeral?) The questions we ask, however, do not turn on virtue merely promised. We know of the commerce in critical discourse, by its own word as fact, not as intent. To ask how that commerce is possible is to leave aside the question of the quantity of its real (or personal) assets. We look rather for the conditions of occurrence, which will be, on the Law of the Conservation of Matter-of-Fact, *matters-of-fact-once-removed. The question, then, first of the manner, as a means to the requisites.*

II Art's Question

Three baseball umpires were comparing accounts. "I call 'em," the first said, "like I see 'em." The second, appealing to the pieties, insisted, "I call 'em like they *are*." The third had simplicity on his side: "Until I call 'em, they ain't."

Overheard in a Third Avenue bar, c. 1950

. . . Though all our knowledge begins with experience, it does not follow that it all arises out of experience.

Kant, Introduction (B) to
Critique of Pure Reason

2

Criticism: Its
Modes and Performance

The end of art criticism must (on grounds of geography if not of logic) reside either inside or outside itself. I shall be attributing to criticism the second of these forms, describing its role as means to an end other than its own expression. For the moment this ulterior purpose is undefined; until the appearances of criticism are themselves in evidence, to represent it as an enabling act of vision is hardly to distinguish criticism from the act of putting on one's glasses, or more simply of opening one's eyes. And that distinction, although not sharp, should be made.

I do not mean out-of-hand to deny an intrinsic justification for criticism. It is possible that a work of art may be assessed simply for the critic's (or the work's) sake. But if we start with what is given (*as* it is given), the characteristic intention of the activity of criticism is apparent. As practice reveals, critical judgment is mediative, the handmaid of another mistress, serving it sometimes faithfully, at other times not, but still poised at the call of a larger comprehension. It attempts finally to evoke a response, to make a difference to its reader, a difference which approximates that of art itself. So construed, the function of criticism follows the lines of the "correction of taste" remarked by writers from Shaftesbury to Eliot. I shall claim, against even some of those accounts, that this correction is open-ended: that in the characteristic attempt to open to the reader the view of what the critic sees in the work of art, the critic's vision, far from simply mirroring or exhibiting the factual properties of the object or of given or inherent standards of taste, is contingent on the inventiveness of taste and its related orders of conceptualization. What the effects of this process of critical suasion are, what it hopes finally to provide access *to*, are questions which may be answered as the process becomes distinct.

This is not to say that criticism is incapable of other functions. Nor does it imply, even if criticism historically reveals features of heteronomy, that we are bound to acknowledge in them the look that criticism ought to have—an important qualification for those who, in the spirit of Matthew Arnold, regard criticism as a moral enterprise. To start with criticism as it is "done," however, is hardly to prescribe its limits. What we do is to start at the beginning of the evidence.

In the discussion which follows I attempt to disclose the grounds for this one very general thesis—that the final end or "cause" of criticism is in fact the end or goal of art—and to outline the consequences of this connection both for criticism and for the process of aesthetic inquiry. The thesis reveals a number of facets, the most important of which is an argument for the "persuasive" character of critical judgment. Admittedly, the context in which that term has gained its recent philosophical currency is that of "persuasive definition," and I shall here ascribe to criticism features of persuasive "judgment." But a paraphrase of the formulation of persuasive definition makes the transition: persuasive judgment is designed to initiate a response (or to revise earlier responses) by calling attention to aspects of an object; the pertinence of those aspects to appreciation of the object are the issues at stake in the critical process; and critical judgment, insofar as it is persuasive, attempts to direct the attitudes of the readers of criticism by proposing (not by demonstrating) as pertinent certain aspects of the object, rather than others.[1] The critical judgment, in other words, is rather an evocation than a representation.

This need not (contrary to at least some of Charles Stevenson's arguments) undermine the objective pretensions of criticism; we shall see the inadequacy, for example, of viewing criticism as essentially or simply "emotive." Furthermore, the critic's motives, although undoubtedly no less venal than those of other pedagogues, are also unlikely to be less various. He tends to his work, we know, because (rarely) he so earns his living; or he attacks, for the sake of the rivalry, a reading subsidized by a rival ideology; he speaks, at another moment, from the exuberance of striking a trace of genius. The intent to persuade recurs, the diversity of motives notwithstanding. If the critic's audience does not eventually find in a work or style the aspects that he notes there, he has lost more than an audience; sufficiently "wrong-headed" to persist, defying them and any possible audience, he assumes the role of solipsistic juror assigning grades to an indifferent universe—a role which essentially denies its own presence. For the critic, success alone succeeds, and nothing fails like failure.

To claim that the purpose of the critic is to win an audience to his manner of seeing, however, is not to imply that he seeks agreement on facts embodied or represented in the work of art; it is a more basic fact still, as I shall argue, that the "facts" to which the critic refers are precisely what are at issue in the critical process. The critic is in effect an agent through whom aspects of the work are articulated (and they become "aspects" as they are articulated); he creates as he "describes," intending that his readers see his creation within the indefinite limits of vision sponsored by the object they all attend to. The critic's world of judgment manages only a tenuous relation to the world of "facts": he is in good measure himself responsible for the second of those worlds as well as for the first, and more basically still, for the relation which joins them.

Such a claim may seem viable only at the expense of common sense. It may quickly be objected, for example, that to characterize critical statements and justifications as persuasive or tendentious skews the very distinction those several terms are meant to fortify. Would it be tendentious to support a critical explanation of the expressive figures in Picasso's painting of Guernica by reference to the bombing in the Spanish Civil War? No more, surely, than if in arguing that it had been raining, one called attention to the wet pavement. These involve circumscribed matters-of-fact and of-inference which are quite different from items of "evidence" calculated to lull (or gull) an audience into admitting something which isn't really the case. Persuasive judgment, after all, specifically does not trade in matters-of-fact; it turns on the attempt to extend concepts by superimposing on them elements whose pertinence the facts by themselves do not establish. And neither of the abbreviated arguments mentioned, this objection might conclude, proceeds in this way.

Well, perhaps. I shall be attempting to show that as it figures in critical judgment, the distinction between "hard" statements of matter-of-fact and persuasive statements is characteristically blurred, and that the judgments of criticism may be significant and corrigible despite this. What such a thesis implies about the more ordinary, garden varieties of judgment is another and longer story.

The Modes of Criticism. Art criticism is frequently identified with the evaluation of works of art. I do not wish to argue what finally may be only the stipulation of a point concerning the usage of a term. But it is clear enough that in both the general (and loose) talk about art and in most writing that falls under the rubric of criticism, a variety of functions is served, and not only, or perhaps not even primarily, that of evaluation.

It will be useful, in testing the thesis so far outlined, to distinguish three modes of criticism—a distinction designed to reflect the principal prima facie differences in critical practice. The distinction itself, then, is also prima facie; a more profound indistinction will become evident later. To the first, "syntactic" form of criticism belong the critic's efforts to name and allocate to categories any part(s) of the work, or even to speak about the work as a whole but in that same restricted sense, for example, as he labels a "mannerist" painting. His concern in this activity takes the form of a question of identification: "*Who* is it?"—the "it" designating putative members of the class cited. What is sought is the contextual identification of the element questioned: its role in the context of accepted usage, historical fact, linguistic rule, etc. This process would naturally end in recognition, the sense of knowing who is who.

The critic working in this mode thus characteristically takes note of and solves obscurities in the art object, for example rendering (as Eliot himself did in "The Waste Land") arcane allusions of a poem, or identifying the figures in a painting on an historical theme. He may attempt to place the whole of the work historically, within the canon of an author or of a style. So, for instance, the statement that Vivaldi was the first composer to give equal importance in his concerti to the slow movement and the two allegros. Other syntactic judgments might speak of what Aristotle in the *Poetics* calls "accidental" errors—the anachronism, for example, of the stage direction "clock strikes" in Shakespeare's *Julius Caesar*. Still other statements in this mode might refer to the relative position or consistency of parts of the work, assessing the balance among vectors of a painting or the psychological plausibility of a dramatic character. The latter are increasingly remote instances of syntactic criticism because although they may only name or identify elements of the art work (works, curves, figures), they come close to the (admittedly vague) line which sets that mode of criticism off from the second one which refers to the "whatness" or import of the work.

Syntactic criticism represents a version of Kant's "determinant" judgment, which Kant defines as the subsumption of a particular instance under a rule independently determined.[2] Independently the critic knows or is able to find out the constitutive elements of the work criticized, the definitions of certain terms, for example, or a pattern of historical circumstance, the biography of the artist, or the generic conventions of a medium. He then invokes these independently established explicators, as principles in terms of which elements of the individual work are identified. Critical procedure in this mode of criticism "determines" an aspect or the instance of the work by establishing its relation to any of the general formulations available in the interpreter's "glossary."

Syntactic criticism, the analysis of the component parts or

syntax of the work of art, is criticism in its most common appearance. At times it verges so closely on the non- or extra-critical uses of determinant judgment that the distinction between them may seem to be without a difference. The conclusions of a critic who has traced the sources of an art work, for example, may appear identical to those of an historian or psychologist analyzing the same object. There are, however, instances of syntactic judgment which clearly reveal the critic speaking in his role as critic; and part of what I am attempting here is to determine how this distinction is sustained. The act of the critic even in translating a Sanskrit word is, I shall argue, characteristically different from that of the etymologist who accomplishes what might superficially seem to be the same end.

The other two modes of criticism respond to characteristically different critical questions from that answered by syntactic judgment. The second mode, "reflective" criticism, involves the interpretation of the work articulated in all of its parts, as the sum which turns out to be more than the dissociated and superficially independent elements to which the first mode attends. It responds to the question of *"What* is it?", what the work amounts to. In raising this question, the critic moves away from the flat surface of identification to the depth structure in which the individual elements discriminated are seen to be articulated with respect to one another and, finally, beyond one another as well. The idiom of this mode of judgment refers (if not always precisely) to the "meaning" of a work, what it expresses or signifies; it takes as a postulate what Northrop Frye speaks of as an "assumption of total coherence" of the work and attempts to determine what the principle of that coherence is.

A distinguishing feature of reflective judgment as against syntactic judgment is that nothing comparable to the rules or glossaries employed by the latter are available to the former as a means; there is no dictionary which can render or determine the whatness of the work. One need assume only a minimal version of the individuality of works of art to recognize the absence of rules by the application of which the meanings of those works can be derived. In cases where such apparently reflective rules apply—

for example, in referring to a film with a "Hollywood ending"—
the work is defective precisely because of that fact. To view the
work as an entity is specifically to go beyond rules previously
determined and is not simply based on the ground that every
entity is unique. The attempt at comprehension is exactly what is
undertaken in practice as the critic attempts to see what the
work, the particular work, is or amounts to. His end, in this mode,
is not categorization but the grasp of a single one.

The comments made so far should not be understood to
mean that the difference between syntactic and reflective
judgment is merely one of scope or that the former achieves a
degree of certainty which the latter does not, although these are
superficial features of the difference. That difference can be
formally located in three related conditions: (a) that reflective
judgments (akin in this regard to theory-laden statements)
employ terms which are not reducible to syntactically determi-
nate elements in the given art work, or even in the general class
of art works; (b) that unlike the status of the art work with
respect to syntactic judgment, the work of art as rendered in
reflective judgment itself contributes to the content of the
principles applied in the process of that judgment; (c) that the
conclusions of reflective judgment involve a characteristic denotative function differing significantly from that of the conclusions
of syntactic judgment. (Examples of these features of reflective
judgment will be seen more fully in the following section.)

The third mode, that of qualitative criticism, includes
judgments in which terms are employed which range from
general value predicates like "good" or "right" to terms more
specifically related to aesthetic quality, like "beautiful" or
"delicate," terms which bear on the worth of the object. Like the
other modes of judgment, this one appears as the answer to the
tacit question: "In what way is the object valuable or not?" or,
more simply, "*How* is it?" Like the other questions referred to,
nothing in the latter makes it peculiarly relevant to aesthetic
objects; it remains to be seen what does mark these questions and
answers as aesthetic. Unlike reflective judgment, qualitative
judgment does not look for a depth structure of articulation;

53

unlike syntactic judgment, its identifications are circumscribed by the distinctive and limited character of the value-identification that it claims.

On some accounts of qualitative judgment (for example, in G. E. Moore's account of beauty as intuitively "seen" [3]), its character hardly differs from that of syntactic judgment. It is sufficient here if we acknowledge only that recognizable prima facie differences (acknowledged also by Moore, as he designates beauty a "non-natural" property) distinguish qualitative judgments from both syntactic and reflective judgments. Certain judgments may remain in dispute: it could be argued whether the judgment of a "delicate" vase, for example, is syntactic or qualitative. But there is a prima facie functional difference among some qualitative and syntactic judgments, as, for example, between "The vase is yellow" and "The vase is beautiful"—a difference in the questions to which they respond and in the kind of knowledge which each assertion conveys.

This threefold allocation to categories of the varieties of critical judgment purports to represent critical practice. The allocation is not intended to limit the expanse of criticism as possible, although it may still be liable to the charge of arbitrariness: it identifies the forms of criticism, but it presumes a knowledge of those forms in fixing the object of its discussion. How do we know, after all, that a given statement is a critical judgment and not a judgment of some other indeterminate kind? There is no external fulcrum to guide this judgment; the only justification for it is that we ordinarily recognize a class of judgments called "critical" which refer to a vaguely defined class of objects and that the assessment of judgments so identified is related to the way they work in practice. Thus, perhaps, it is a circle, but not a vicious one. It is, after all, a matter of fact that the questions claimed above as underlying the several modes of criticism are asked about art.

A final and overriding qualification should preface the more formal account of the modes of criticism which follows. The fact that several modes of criticism may be distinguished on prima facie grounds does not imply their autonomy with respect to each other. The emphasis of the argument here will be on the hierarchical and interlocking relations among the modes, a phenomenon which, it will be argued, plays a more fundamental role in the structure of criticism than do the apparent differences. The grounds for this claim are foreshadowed in the outline I have given of such differences. For example, the critic who in carrying on the process of syntactic criticism explicates an ambiguous term or phrase will, if not invariably, in some cases unavoidably rest his conclusions on the application of reflective judgment to the work in question. Thus, when Hamlet tells Ophelia to "get [her] to a nunnery," the fact that "nunnery" was used colloquially in Shakespeare's England to designate a brothel as well as the dwelling of a religious order could be ascertained by anyone interested in the linguistic usage of the period. But that this ambiguity in the meaning of "nunnery" and not either definition *alone* marks Hamlet's statement could be forcefully asserted only in the light of reflective judgment and by a critic who had admitted the play as a whole to be the thing. The detail of this hierarchical pattern, with its suggestion of the critical priority of reflective judgment, remains to be elaborated.

The Structure of Reflective Judgment. I have claimed that the reflective judgments of criticism respond to the question of *"what* the work (as art) is," and that they differ from syntactic judgments, which only identify or name the work or its parts. To reach the conclusions of syntactic judgment—for instance, by translating the Sanskrit phrases in *The Waste Land* or by identifying the figures in Leonardo's *Last Supper*—demands no more than the use of a "dictionary": the phrases or figures are fully rendered when pertinent rules adduced from sources external to the works are applied. Such rules have at least the weight of conventions and usually something more; and although the judgments based on them are sometimes disputable, more often they go almost without saying. Comprehension of the work of art, of what the whole amounts to, can depend on no such indices. The transparency of the process of identification does not extend to the relations of the elements identified with respect to one another. Inclusive or rule-like categories may appear to be pertinent in some judgments of the art work as a whole—generic criteria, for example, like "picaresque" or "sonata," which in the manner of dictionary definitions set sharp limits to critical expectation and understanding. But these categories are short-hand forms for sets of syntactic elements; like the latter, they leave open the question of the work's import.[4]

This point of difference makes the correspondingly divergent question of the origin and structure of reflective judgment a perplexing one—not the question of why it is sought (the origin of its search for larger understanding, one that conceives of the work as a whole or entity, is tied to the origin of the search for *any* understanding),[5] but the question of how it is formed. The following instances of reflective judgment provide a basis for the formal analysis required to answer the latter question. In his essay on *Little Dorrit*, Trilling concludes that in that novel the "whole energy of the imagination is directed to the transcending of the personal will, to the search for the Will in which shall be our peace." [6] This, we are to understand, is what is yielded by the accumulation of elements which have otherwise been identified in the work, its episodes, conversations, and descriptions. It is most important for understanding the logic of reflective judgment to note that this statement nowhere appears in *Little Dorrit* itself. (This is not to say that it could not have appeared there, but only that it does not and that even if it did appear there, that appearance would not mark it as an instance of reflective judgment.) Rather the statement stands apart from the items of syntactic judgment, designed to comprehend the syntactic elements and the judgments which they themselves yield. Trilling gives examples of those other elements; the difference between them and the overarching reflective judgment is instructive. He repeats, for instance, Dickens's description of Daniel Doyce, the inventor frustrated by the bureaucracy of the patent registry, yet persistent in his craft:

> His dismissal of himself was unremarkable. He never said, I discovered this adaptation or invented that combination; but showed the whole

thing as if the Divine Artificer had made it, and he had happened to find it. So modest was he about it, such a pleasant touch of respect was mingled with his quiet admiration of it, and so calmly convinced was he that it was established in irrefrangible laws.

This description comprises a single group of sentences in the novel. To understand or identify them (and Trilling takes this process for granted) requires only an application of independently determined rules governing the vocabulary and rules of usage. The description of Daniel Doyce is thus a syntactic element which could be grasped by anyone familiar only with such rules. The reflective judgment, although related to the other, has quite a different status. It presupposes the identification of the other, syntactic element (for one) and attempts to bring out the relation between that element and the others which have been similarly identified. In attributing to *Little Dorrit* a certain assertive theme, Trilling draws on syntactic components like the description cited; in fact, his conclusion tacitly purports to take account of *all* such components, both those which support it and any others which may conflict with it. (The latter are assumed not to be overriding.) The readers of *Little Dorrit*, Trilling suggests, should see in it a theme beyond the rule-governed elements which appear, a theme which at once takes those elements into account and renders them comprehensible, but which is not itself simply there, as they are.

A second example of this formal difference between reflective and syntactic judgment is evident in Wittkower's analysis of Bernini's *Mary Magdalene* and *St. Jerome*.[7] His statements on these works can be separated into two groups. In the first he writes:

> . . . the figures show two different aspects of this religious attitude of penitence: Mary Magdalene, contrition and remorse, Jerome, mystical surrender. . . . Her face mirrors the despair of her soul, but her eyes turn toward heaven hopeful of salvation. . . . Compositionally a counterpart, the figure of St. Jerome is conceived spiritually as a contrast to the Magdalene: instead of outpoured feelings his mind is turned inwards.

57

These statements contrast with others, interspersed among them, in which Wittkower designates the syntactic components of the sculpture:

> Mary Magdalene's left foot is groping, dragged along the ground, but the right foot rests firmly on the jar of ointment (the customary attribute with which she had anointed the Saviour). Her head rests . . . on her . . . clasped hands. . . . Like Mary Magdalene, St. Jerome places one foot on his attribute, the lion. . . . Bernini, however, departed from the tradition in one important respect. Jerome's head . . . leans against the Cross. . . . According to the law of gravity the Cross could never be in the position in which we see it; for the fingers of the left hand touch the cross-beam without supporting it, while the right hand is clasping the drapery and not the foot of the Cross.

This second group of statements describes common objects and qualities and might be understood or initiated by anyone familiar with the conventions of artistic representation and certain commonplace facts. They can be verified in the same way that a statement about the heights or weights of the sculpted figures might be, by instruments and indices of translation determined independently of any particular application. Thus, they differ from the first set of statements in the same way that the second quotation from Trilling's account of *Little Dorrit* differs from the first one: for each of the pairs, one may or may not agree to the point of its first member, and this openness in the first statements is not due to critical whimsy, but to the absence of an external ground from which to move. Reflective judgments are inferences of a sort (although not deductive inferences), drawn from the syntactic elements cited (the position of the cross, Daniel Doyce's attitude) as well as from other sources which do not appear in the work at all. What is "given" in the Chigi Chapel are two figures set in different postures. The reflective judgment which Wittkower derives from these items of evidence yields perception of a different order. The viewer sees Mary Magdalene's foot; he hardly "sees" the contriteness which the foot (for one) suggests in the same way. We read in *Little*

Dorrit a statement about Daniel Doyce's persistence; and we find that Trilling infers from that statement an assertion of the importance of character which overcomes selfullness not only for Daniel Doyce, but for individual experience that extends beyond the characters of *Little Dorrit*—finally, for the experience of the reader himself.

The first of the three distinguishing features of reflective judgment cited above was that certain terms in such judgment lack direct syntactic reference. That a color in a painting is yellow can be settled by empirical, even mechanical, inspection of the object. An analogous operation would verify Wittkower's assertion that it is Mary Magdalene's right foot which rests on the jar of ointment. The terms employed in reflective judgment—in the examples given: contriteness, transcendence of the will—in contrast, are open to neither this degree nor quality of confirmation. For example, we may claim that we "see" the contriteness in a face; and in certain instances, the process of perception may be no less rapid or confident than when it identifies a color. But the difference between the two forms of judgment is less a matter of time required for making them than of the process by which they emerge.

One way of formulating that difference is found in the claim that no set of necessary and sufficient conditions implies, as by the perception of the motion of an arm, such reflective terms as contriteness. It might be argued that this is also true *in fact* with respect to the identification of a color; but the obvious response to this is that a set of conditions *could* be determined that would establish or refute that identification. This does not deny all connection between syntactic elements and the conclusions of reflective judgment; it asserts only that whatever the connection, it is not deductive in character. One can meaningfully ask, for any alleged or like instance of contriteness, whether some item of evidence not initially considered does not alter the claim for its presence: the concept is defeasible. However, to specify a certain wave length of light is within certain limits to foreclose discussion as to whether the color at issue is yellow.

The analogy referred to previously between the structure of

reflective judgment and that of theoretical statement bears on this point. The syntactic elements of scientific judgment, such as measurements, are subject to empirical verification; but theoretical conclusions based on those measurements have no such consistent foundation. This much, at least, has come clear in the history of unsuccessful attempts to reconcile the structure of scientific theory with a strict empiricist criterion of verification.[8] It seems, in other words, a feature of scientific theories and bound to their explanatory role that they employ constructs for which there is evidence, yet which are not themselves open to the kind of scrutiny to which that evidence itself is. A similar discrepancy holds, I have been suggesting, in the relation between syntactic and reflective judgments of art criticism. The totality of syntactic elements enumerable in a work of art, each identified by its place in a rule-governed context, does not exhaust the referents of reflective terms which pertain to them.

This conclusion is related closely to the second feature of reflective judgment: namely, that the principles applied in the judgment are affected, in an important sense generated through, the judgment itself. In contrast to the rules and structures adduced in deriving syntactic judgments—dictionary definitions, descriptions of historical background, patterns of tonal relations —which appear to exist independently of the particular critical context, the autonomy of reflective principles is limited. They may in historical fact have begun to emerge prior to any particular one of their applications; but the justification for applying them is in every case in quality identical to the justification for their original formulation. To discern somebody as contrite, be it a person or a figure in a painting, is to have remarked an aspect in certain syntactic cues.[9] That aspect is a function of the cues; the evidence which led to awareness of the aspect initially or to the formulation of a concept based on it, although scattered in place and time, is of the same order as the evidence or cues displayed in the object being newly observed. Its status in any particular instance is as firmly or shakily grounded as it has ever been. This is not a situation where the multiplication of instances contributes to "confirmation," any more than, in Wittgenstein's example, we would expect to check the accuracy of a newspaper story by looking at another copy of the same edition. In remarking the aspect of contrition, the critic is also devising it to the extent, at least, that he has ever devised or discovered it. The material which underwrites the aspect or concept is given in the particular work, or in other works or objects which are in that respect indistinguishable from the one now addressed. The aspect to which reflective judgment attests can thus never be identified by the application of an independent set of rules for the very good reason that no such rules exist. This does not mean that the aspect discerned is not in some sense "there"; it means only that (also in some sense) its presence is postulated or contrived. How this is accomplished remains to be seen.

The third distinguishing feature of reflective judgment is its denotative status. The peculiarities of that status are exemplified in the proposal of Trilling's as he discerns in *Little Dorrit* the theme that peace comes only with escape from the domination of the will, not only as that theme is represented for a character in the novel but as it extends in force beyond both him and it. To identify a figure in a painting, for example in the syntactic judgment that "The second figure from the right is St. Peter," is to denote by that judgment's predicate a circumscribed object or in other cases a quality. Such objects or qualities are complete in the sense that they have a spatial and/or temporal location or definition independent of the critic as well as of the work: so, for example, St. Peter the man. The terms of reflective judgment, however, denote a general class. It is Escape-from-the-Domina-tion-of-the-Will of which Trilling speaks, not a particular escape from the domination of the will. That class, furthermore, has a singularly active modal status; it is not historically fixed, but rather opens out even as it is "denoted" beyond the extent of its source and beyond the past or present which in a sheer material sense have fixed it in place. The object of Trilling's claim refers not to a static or abstract mental state or action, but to a process in which the unfolding projection of the reader is itself an element. This distinctive aspect of the denotation of reflective judgment, although related to the two other conditions mentioned, requires a more elaborate exposition of its own (see chapter 3).

Enough has been said, notwithstanding the postponement of discussion of the last condition, to indicate the grounds for construing reflective judgment as persuasive. Persuasive judgment effects an understanding or way of seeing which the facts by themselves do not command; it proposes revision or expansion in perception without justifying either its means or the conclusions reached. And this statement affords a convenient summary of the practice of reflective judgment. The conclusions to which reflective judgment points are not given in the work; nor are they available independently of the work. Rather they are "taken" by the critic, who then asks the reader to view the art work through the medium of organization which his articulation provides. The content and application of that medium is the critic's primary concern; his justification comes not from reference to the "facts of the matter," since for this matter, there *are* no facts, at least no decisive facts, but from his recommendation that the work of art can fruitfully be regarded in a certain way. Whatever else it may be in its parts, we know beforehand that a judgment which incorporates a recommendation is not simply a recognition of matters of fact. The critic does not see the assertion of the value of the transcendence of the will as he sees the words which make up *Little Dorrit*. But he makes sense of the words which he sees by devising that concept and subsuming them under it. The source, or part of the source, of the concept is in the sensibility that applies it. As the concept is applied, the critic proposes for his audience a redirection of sensibility on the grounds, finally, of his own.

According to this step in the argument, then, the categories by which the work of art is grasped are elicited in an important measure from the object to which they are applied. The critic initially faces the syntactic facts of the work of art (color, dictionary meaning, etc.) as well as the facts of other indirectly related abstractions (commonsense generalizations, scientific theories, other critical statements, ideologies) in terms of which he structures his view of the former. But reflective principles of intelligibility for the individual work of art, so long as the work is not simply derivative or academic, do not appear among those recognizable facts. The critic, if he succeeds, conceives a principle under which data of the art work—meanings of individual words, figures, tonal relations—come alive, are pertinent, make sense in terms of the whole. But he conceives this sense, he does not find it; he construes it rather than recognizes it, and then recommends that conception—his conception—to his audience.

An obvious question concerning reflective criticism so defined concerns its verification. The description given suggests that the process leading to reflective judgment is oval if not circular. Such judgment obtains its force as the features which it reveals in the object support it; the features support it, not surprisingly, because the principles of the judgment itself have defined them. To defend Trilling's reflective judgment on *Little Dorrit*, for example, is in the last resort to fall back on the assertion that the set of features to which he relates the concept of self-effacement "has the look" that self-effacement has. And if we ask how one knows what that look is or that the case referred to is an example of that look, the only response available is to point to the same phenomenon again or to other instances of the look which have no greater cogency as evidence but only a different ambience than does the instance cited.

It may seem to follow from this analysis that there are no checks on the claims of reflective criticism, that all of those claims must be judged equally adequate or fruitful. And, in fact, an indefinite number of alternate reflective judgments are logically possible. As the most dubious scientific hypothesis might be defended through the giving up of other, less dubious hypotheses and/or through the disputing of particular syntactic facts, so it is possible to affirm any reflective judgment at the expense of other judgments, reflective or not. One could, for example, dispute Wittkower's interpretation based on the position of the cross if before this one disputed his presuppositions on the nature of gravity. And as Wittkower assumes the conventional properties of gravity in his version of the import of the pieces of sculpture, one could, in rejecting his description of those properties, argue (for example, from the nonexistence of gravity) to conflicting judgments about their import.

The range of possibilities opened by this account does not, however, give free range to the critic. For one thing, there is no special reason to exempt him from the cutting edge of Ockham's razor. It may be a pertinent question in general as to why, of two accounts, the one which makes both the fewer and the lesser assumptions is to be preferred; and there may be some question in any particular case as to how those assumptions are to be measured. Nevertheless, the art critic is no freer from responsibility to the principle of conceptual economy than anyone else. His interest as critic will undoubtedly be with a limited segment and type of experience; but if we acknowledge a relation among the varieties of experience, he can hardly ask forbearance to bring order into one of its moments at the expense of creating disorder for others which are no less fundamental—for example, by introducing a psychoanalytic interpretation that is inconsistent with psychoanalytic principles. There is therefore this internal homeostasis which serves the critic as limit and which serves his critic as a criterion for evaluating the critic's conclusions.

This contextual standard admittedly provides only a negative check on the range of reflective judgment and by implication leaves the critic considerable latitude. It is true, furthermore (tautologically), that at no point in criticism will the critic know the object as it "really" is (as it is unknown to him); nor can the evidence ever adequately determine what a "genuine" or characteristically human response to a particular stimulus is or what an aesthetic object *ought* to be. Yet substantial, if not logically tight, grounds can be given even within these limits for the assessment of critical judgments.

The Subordination of Qualitative and Syntactic Judgment. It has been important procedurally to draw a preliminary distinction between (a) reflective judgment and (b) qualitative and syntactic judgment. In introducing that distinction, however, I suggested that its parts contained common and hierarchically ordered elements. I now mean to suggest that the persuasive character of reflective judgment, as a consequence of that judgment's logical priority to the others, is also a dominant feature of syntactic and qualitative judgment. So far as this is the case, whatever the differences between reflective judgment and the others, there will be a fundamental congruence among the varieties of judgments which takes its character from reflective judgment. To argue this point is to qualify severely the distinction originally drawn: the prima facie differences give way before the more basic and common features of critical judgment as such.

Of the three modes of critical judgment, qualitative judgment presents itself, in certain traditional accounts, as most evidently persuasive. To give reasons for the claim that an object is valuable, or even to make the bare assertion, has often been construed as a means for the expression of an attitude for which neither the speaker nor his audience, even if they agree, can give factual justification. On almost any analysis of the descriptive modes of discourse, where hard facts stand at one end of a spectrum, qualitative terms stand at the other, if they are not quite off it. Stevenson's analysis of persuasive definition, it will be recalled, originated in his study of value judgments. This predisposition lends immediate plausibility to the reduction of qualitative to reflective judgment. It is important to note, however, that the emotivist account of judgment has its own varieties and that the form ascribed here to qualitative criticism (and thus, by implication, to criticism in general) is a sharply limited version.

It is indisputable that a radical emotivist analysis[10] provides an adequate rendering of some instances of qualitative judgment. Certain uses of "x is beautiful," for example, undoubtedly are expressions of approval, implying no more about the object than that in some undefined way it pleases the viewer; such judgments could be replaced with no loss by a smile or some other telltale nonverbal expression. This reduction is not universally adequate, however, and exceptional cases are the more in evidence as qualitative judgment becomes increasingly specific. To speak, for example, of a good sonnet implies the existence of criteria for measuring the object at least in its structure as a sonnet.[11] There is no way to disagree with a smile; but the reader who refers to a rondeau as a sonnet—good *or* bad—is flatly mistaken. There may be disputes about what class a particular object belongs to, even with respect to the class of art itself as when we ask whether something is art at all; and there may be disputes about what the characteristics are which define a particular class. But in a large number of cases, such disputes do not arise: we could hardly mistake a good sonnet for a good drawing, or for a bad drawing either.

It may be objected that this qualification on the principal theme of emotivism only temporizes with the conclusions of that theory concerning what the "goodness" of the sonnet finally amounts to. Certainly the burden of the issue is there; but we have also to keep in view the contextual use of "good," which is a constant, and perhaps even the most basic, feature of qualitative predicates. Such contextual grounds figure, for example, in predicates like "delicate," "garish," "deft": each is a function of, if not strictly deducible from, syntactic properties. If we know certain syntactic properties of a vase, we also know with a fair measure of probability the applicability to it of the qualitative property "delicate." That probability begins with such gross syntactic predicates as linear measurements: a vase with a bowl whose diameter is one foot, whose stem has a circumference of three inches and a height of one inch is not likely, we could agree even without seeing it, to be delicate.[12] Again, the critic who describes the relative width and coloring of the lines in Rouault's paintings to someone who has not seen them, and then refers to them as "tentative" or "fragile," could be known by the other either to have his faculty of judgment distorted or to understand those terms in such a way that their more common usage must be revised. And this conclusion would emerge not in the presence of a particular work of art, but from what is known generally of art, as well as aside from art altogether.

It is impossible to draw up an a priori list of syntactic properties and the corresponding qualitative predicates for which they would serve as necessary and sufficient conditions. But a deductive model of that relation is not the only one possible. On an inductive model, the relation between the two types of predicate is both coherent and evident—a point strongly attested if we attempt to conceive of qualitative predicates *not* grounded in syntactic ones. For we find here that qualitative predicates require an underpinning of syntactic elements; without that underpinning the ascription of qualitative predicates can have no significance. To imagine a "garish" combination of colors in the absence of particular colors is, quite simply, impossible. This claim should not be taken for a positive statement of a version of intuitionism (like that, for example, of Roger Fry) which assigns to qualitative predicates the same objective status as syntactic predicates. I assume the irrelevance of this position if only because the intuitionist claims a last court of appeal which is denied his audience, arguing that he sees facts, with the power of intuition, to which his critics are blind. There is no refuting such claims because there is no way of dealing with them at all.

These comments indicate what in qualitative judgment marks its relation to and dependence on reflective judgment. In each of the cases cited, the qualitative predicates involve syntactic elements: that a given poem is a good sonnet implies as a condition of that goodness, that it has fourteen lines, a fixed rhyme pattern, etc. But it is also apparent that such judgments of goodness refer to more than only syntactic characteristics. Implied is the fact not only that the poem meets the requirements for being a sonnet, but that meeting those requirements itself has value and that sonnets themselves are in some way a good. There seems, in other words, as one parses the idiom of qualitative judgment, an incipient drive beyond the identification of the object judged. Reference to a delicate vase not only assigns the object to the class of vases but suggests that its delicacy, and delicate vases, are worth attending to: the judgment is also a recommendation.

This general claim concerning the commendatory status of qualitative judgment can be established by a *reductio* argument. If it were not the case, there would be no incongruity in the

67

statement that "the lines of this vase are delicate, but that is no reason, everything else being equal, for anyone to look at it." And there is something incongruous about that claim. The same commendatory element is evident, moreover, as one extends the range of examples. We speak of a "profoundly moving string quartet," of a "fine baroque church," or of the "graceful balance in a drawing." It is evident that the speaker in each such case intends to do something more than place an object in a class. There may be no foolproof means of demonstrating this for a particular instance; there are instances of similar formulations of judgment—"That's a good example of paranoid behavior"—for which the thesis holds only in an attenuated sense. But the weight of usage in the context of aesthetic judgment is imposing.

Certain implications emerge from these comments concerning the relation between qualitative and syntactic judgments. Close to their intersection, we may speak, for example, of a garish painting. Whether we construe "garish" either as a qualitative or as a syntactic predicate, it is context-bound. We would be unlikely to speak of a garish sonata, not because sonatas are without faults, but because that quality is, by and large, irrelevant to its contextual possibilities. However, a painting and a sonata may each be referred to as beautiful. For this more general level of qualitative judgment, dependence on syntactic elements and generic context has been substantially diminished; whatever other element sponsors qualitative judgment has become proportionately stronger. It is this other element, its peculiar commendatory aspect, for which qualitative judgment is indebted to reflective judgment. To say that "x is beautiful" would not ordinarily be understood to mean that "x is beautiful of its kind" (if the latter statement makes sense at all). Perhaps it will be argued that in designating something as beautiful, we refer that quality to the context of "things," but there is little informative in this reference or in the statement itself if this is what it is supposed to mean. A radical emotivist account would infer from this apparent diminution in its syntactic ground that the judgment is then more obviously one which merely expresses certain feelings. But this extreme alternative, I hope to show, is neither implied by the evidence nor adequate to it.

For the moment the question is not whether "beautiful" or other similarly general qualitative predicates may not be analogical or even equivocal: there seem in fact obvious differences in meaning among the beautiful landscape, the beautiful painting of the landscape, the beautiful necklace, etc. What is at issue is whether such terms have some common reflective function that might allow, in its least syntactically-related appearances, for the absence of contextual reference without implying by that absence a lapse into subjectivism. That such a function is likely becomes evident if we recall the aspects ascribed earlier to reflective judgment. Through reflective judgment the critic finds the whole of a work to possess a character which, as he confronts the work's individual elements, exerts the force of an overarching and regulative principle. In explicating that principle he marks off a point of view which yields a particular appreciation of the object; he in effect asks his audience to *see* the object or aspect—and "seeing" here stands metaphorically for the varieties of experience which include both feeling and knowing—in a certain way. At a minimum, the representation of an aspect of the object figures in his judgment; that representation, at the same time, makes an overture beyond the work to its other, prospective viewers.

This persuasive feature of reflective judgment also holds, it now turns out, for qualitative judgment. The function of qualitative judgments may seem to differ from that of the reflective judgments cited, insofar as the latter involved primarily discursive themes. That the critic may communicate less fully what he means by "beautiful" than he does in outlining more specific concepts like that which Trilling derives from *Little Dorrit*, however, is less to the point than is their common critical appearance. In both usages the critic raises a possibility of experience for his reader. In neither case is that possibility fixed by an external or prior point of reference. In both cases it is difficult for the reader who has not in some related form recognized what the critic identifies to grasp what he says; in neither case can the critic so fully detail what he means that critical success is assured. The fact of aesthetic value, like that of aesthetic substance, is irretrievably contingent.

It may be objected against these supposed parallels that to understand Trilling's reference to self-transcendence, for example, is to have learned or reaffirmed the meaning of a phrase, but that to understand what a critic means in speaking of beauty is to learn or to be persuaded into an experience. But the distinction is strained. Trilling, in his role as critic, defines a connection between the impression made by a work of art and a conceptual principle. To speak of an object as beautiful narrows considerably the range of the principle applied, but it does not avoid the use of such principle. Precisely how we learn to apply the concepts of beauty or aesthetic value, or to circumscribe the experience which they designate, is a large question; but it is itself part of a still larger question of how we ever learn to discriminate among, or to "have," moments of experience. Whatever the answer to this, one facet of it is clear: the claims that qualitative predicates such as beauty are either given (like syntactic predicates) or projected as expressions of the viewer conflict with the actual practice of critical judgment. Neither the role of critic nor that of the reader of criticism would be comprehensible if either of these alternatives were the case. The critic, judging the work qualitatively, points beyond the facts of the object, incorporating them into a larger comprehension; he contributes a principle of comprehension, a reflective principle, developed in the refinement of his own appreciation of art. That principle, grounded finally in terms of beauty or aesthetic values, remains like other reflective predicates defeasible; like them it has finally to be seen to be believed. The beauty or aesthetic value of any particular object almost certainly is not a single discriminable property of the object; the elements of judgment by which it is articulated are similarly complex, even indefinite. But this does not distinguish them fundamentally from other elements and principles involved in reflective judgment. A common error in thinking about value predicates has been to assume that since they serve apparently distinctive functions, they have correspondingly different formal origins from what have been called here reflective predicates; Beauty seems remote indeed from meaning. It should be evident, moreover, from what has been said that a judgment on the one hardly implies a judgment on the other, although surely at some point they touch. The point that I have been arguing with respect to their relation is only that their conceptual origins and ultimately their functions are formally related.

This account may still appear, on essential points, to resemble and even to reinforce the emotivist critique of value; but the differences are greater than the similarities. To say that qualitative judgment goes beyond the facts discernible in an object judged does not imply that there is no connection between the judgment and the facts. A variety of evidence argues for that connection, not the least among which are the objections to its denials: the "Naturalistic Fallacy" is no fallacy and in its original formulation hardly even a clear statement of the position it criticizes.[13] Judgments on the beautiful do not occur at random, as projections merely of a critic's needs or wishes; nor, when they do occur, need they be taken or left as they stand. They can be argued, and although no one can deduce someone else into an experience, perception is educable. Precisely how qualitative judgments manage not to be arbitrary has been hinted at in reference to the question of verification as it applies to reflective judgment; that problem is discussed further below. But the parallel between qualitative and reflective judgment is so far clear. There are no necessary and sufficient conditions for the predicate "beautiful," any more than there are for "delicate." Like the discriminated elements that support the judgment of a vase as delicate, syntactic elements also sponsor the broader reaches of qualitative judgment. The most specific ground for this claim appears in such qualitative phrases as a "good example of baroque architecture" or the "most beautiful of Shakespeare's sonnets" where the terms have an obvious contextual base; these examples are symptomatic of all the appearances of qualitative judgment. In their persuasive and reflective character, however, qualitative judgments go beyond the syntactic elements of the art work. At the point where reflective and qualitative predicates converge, one finds the last source of the concepts projected by them both. The means by which we grasp or apply them may differ: we feel aesthetic value differently from the way in which we feel the contriteness projected in a painting. But, as phenomena, the two types of predicate reveal themselves at the outcome of formally similar processes, offering the viewer a purchase on the object which its elements, by themselves and unarticulated, would not. Qualitative judgment, it might be put differently, is a sensuous manifestation of reflective judgment. The syntactic elements which induce it are the counterparts of the elements which support nonqualitative, reflective judgments.

The account thus far does not refute the emotivist critique of qualitative judgment (it is difficult, in fact, to know from the terms of that critique how it could be refuted); but it undercuts it, although at the same time holding still to the persuasive character of qualitative judgment. The judgment of an object as beautiful—both the act and the statement—superimposes a new aspect on the object to which the judgment contributes and which in itself the object would not have contrived. To judge an object as aesthetically valuable is to have perceived it, to have experienced it in a certain way by at the same time organizing a structure which makes perception or experience possible. There are a number of necessary and sufficient conditions which determine that a given piece of writing is a sonnet. Those conditions might be applied by a reader who knew nothing of poetry and perhaps not even the language in which the sonnet was written. But to say of the same piece that it is a good sonnet presupposes a direct measure and quality of experience, whatever the terms in which that experience is defined. Reflective principles supervene on this qualitative judgment, projecting the concept and content of aesthetic value as they do in eliciting the work's more discursive import. Reflective judgment thus embodies both what are commonly titled interpretation and evaluation. Formally, they are aspects of the same process, arrived at by the same means.

The strongest contrast drawn so far among the modes of

criticism has been claimed between syntactic and reflective judgment. That contrast is superficially quite plausible; yet, for all its usefulness as a marking distinction, it gives way at a more fundamental level to a convergence not dissimilar to that of qualitative and reflective judgment. This second convergence appears despite the dependence of syntactic judgment on rules of classification whose status, unlike those employed in reflective judgment, appear to be independent of the judgment itself. It may seem to strain the limits of usage to characterize the translation of certain phrases from the Sanskrit or the fact that Shakespeare's *Hamlet* was or was not based on Thomas Kyd's work as manifestations of reflective judgment. Certainly, if there were instances of critical judgment in which independent principles drawn from outside the aesthetic context determined the judgment, we would find them here. Yet a difference does exist between such statements of facts in their role as etymology, historical statement, or analysis by the psychology of art, on the one hand, and as they figure in art criticism, on the other. It is that difference which assures the common bond between syntactic and reflective judgment.

Neither the critic nor the historian, it seems fair to generalize, would be interested in a statement about the relation between Shakespeare and Kyd for its own sake, isolated and out of context (if such a statement were possible at all). For each the description of the origins of *Hamlet* is meant to serve an end which determines not only the process leading to the statement but the statement's meaning as well. One central "meaning of meaning" is that of function. Saying that "this is a good one" after looking through the novels in one's library to select a window prop means something different (perhaps something identical as well—but also something different) from what is meant in the superficially identical statement made by a literary juror as he evaluates the same collection of novels. It is irrelevant for the moment how such distinctions come to be known; what is important is that to ignore or to deny them is also to mistake the meanings of the various judgments which, viewed literally, employ identical terms.

It hardly begs the question concerning the hierarchy of the roles of criticism to claim as a premise that the enterprise of criticism is concerned finally with the appreciation of works of art, with the import of those works as entities. The formal aspects of this largest sense of aesthetic appreciation will be dealt with more fully below; the premise itself, however, discloses the grounds of connection between syntactic and reflective judgment. The implication follows from the premise that what qualifies syntactic judgment as criticism at all is its subscription to some larger governing principle which establishes the former's relevance to the appreciation of the work. Factual syntactic statements made about the object (describing even such properties as weight, width) become critical judgments as they are seen and shown by the critic to clarify effectively a projection of the work as such, as an aesthetic whole. The critic may not demonstrate this consequence explicitly or in each instance of syntactic explication; but it is crucial and it is implied in his project that he should be able to do so. The isolated elements of syntactic judgment make sense in the long run of criticism only as the long run itself makes sense critically. To speak of the most limited syntactic judgment as if it were self-generating and beyond *any* context misrepresents the nature of judgment in general and critical judgment in particular. If syntactic judgments are less revealing than the other types of critical judgment with respect to the whole of the object on which they focus, that whole becomes evident only as the critic, looking for comprehension, adduces certain syntactic elements in that process. But he turns to the latter as a consequence of the drive for reflective judgment and its articulation. The substantive relation between the two types of judgment, then, is dialectical: each gives content to the other. But the formal priority belongs to reflective judgment.

So far as reflective judgment is persuasive or tendentious, syntactic judgment, which is formally dependent on it, assumes the same character. The "facts" of the art work are adduced or preserved only as the principles of reflective judgment determine the relevance of such facts. And as those reflective principles are characteristically persuasive, as they act beyond the domain of the hardest facts, so, by implication, are the judgments to which they lead. Reflective judgment, again, may seem remote from the simple and apparently factual statement that *Hamlet* was completed in 1601. That statement, in any particular use, might not be identified as an instance of criticism; nor does it, like reflective judgment, purport immediately to persuade the reader of a force extending beyond the historical fact. But so far as it is intended to effect a particular understanding of *Hamlet*, then the detail itself—which out of that context may seem a brute fact—is, in context, no less persuasive than the larger judgment to which it leads or gives support. And this is a claim not only about the function but about the brute status of the "fact" itself. That fact acquires its status as criticism on the basis of the nature of the critical enterprise. The facts of the art work as art work thus cannot be assumed to be identical with the facts of the art work as physical object or historical object or psychological object to which different principles, determined by their different ends, apply; nor can they be analyzed in terms of a context-free set of facts, the very existence of which would be problematic on this account as it might be enlarged. It may be difficult at times to determine whether or how specific instances of syntactic judgment contribute to aesthetic intelligibility; but such questions can themselves be resolved only as we go beyond syntactic judgment itself. The apparent facts of syntactic judgment, so far as they affect the process of criticism, do not even exist apart from the prior impulse and discrimination provided by reflective judgment. Whether such facts ever achieve independence or autonomy is a separate (and problematic) question.

Criticism as Performance. It may seem that not very much is gained even if the account given of reflective judgment were accepted: that by it the limits of critical judgment appear so attenuated and remote from the work of art that the concrete presence of art itself is lost; second, that it is in any event no more compelling than the general theory of meaning which it evidently presupposes but which has not been argued. The former of these contentions may be disputed, however, not by denying the formal quality of the account of reflective judgment but on the ground that if reflective judgment holds the key to the character of any particular item of criticism, there should be nothing surprising about the general force that has been ascribed to it. The test of that generality will be in how the concept serves—whether the actual practice of criticism is made intelligible by it. The second objection has more weight. There is little question that at stake finally in any analysis of critical discourse will be a general theory of meaning or utterance. In speaking about the logical status of critical judgment, I shall attempt to make explicit the points at which the discussion impinges on such a theory.

A third and more immediately pressing objection to the account of reflective judgment might be that the character which it apparently gives to the whole of art criticism suggests a mode of discourse itself closed to criticism. The structure of critical judgment appears unstable in a way that other types of judgment are apparently not, lacking grounds on which its assertions rest or against which they can be measured. The harder the facts adduced in critical judgment, one might even infer from what has been said, the less pertinent or suggestive they will be to the central impulse of criticism. Criticism, it seems to turn out, is a variation on the arts on which it is supposed to wait, and the critic is an artist, referring his work to principles which are neither explicit nor corrigible. He devises those principles at the same time that he applies them; the evidence used to support his conclusions turns out to be part of the conclusions. Criticism then takes on the look of a Pandora's box that promises a conglomeration of the fantasies of its practitioners.

This prospect is unavoidable, and the history of criticism contributes to the impression. Critical judgments have repeatedly proved to be very much in and of the contingent world. Reputations and the judgments which make them, we know, have risen and fallen and will continue to do so; the "pot of paint thrown by a coxcomb in the face of the public" of one generation finds its way to a museum in a later one; the writer taken at the apex of his career to be the "twentieth-century Dickens" turns out, not much later in that century, to be the considerably more modest Hugh Walpole. The meaning, no less than the value of aesthetic objects, may expand markedly in time, and (although this is less easy to demonstrate) other significance is surely lost. Whatever the cave paintings of Lascaux and Altamira tell us, we may safely assume a difference from their significance in the life of their original audience. Thus, to conceive of criticism as an explication of the facts of art, as science is sometimes construed as an explication of the facts of nature, seems a mistake or at best a simplification both on historical grounds, and on the systematic grounds outlined earlier. The historical fluctuations in critical understanding reinforce the thesis that the statements of criticism are not merely descriptions of qualities or aspects that wait to be noticed.

At the same time, however, I have argued that the emotivist account which renders critical judgments as expressions or imperatives reflecting the critic's moods, is also defective. Even superficially, and aside from the systematic account given, there seems more in reflective judgment than the involuntary reflex or discharge which emoting would sometimes suggest;[14] the history of critical understanding and evaluation, although a history of revision and discovery, is not simply chaotic. In confronting the objections cited, then, we must face the question of the logical status of critical judgment. The requirements of such an analysis are twofold: first, the formulation of a theory of linguistic usage which may serve as a ground for the analysis of critical judgment given above; second, the delineation, in that theory, of controls by which individual critical judgments may be assessed. The former of these requirements, for obvious reasons, cannot be fully met here; I shall attempt only to suggest an account which answers to it in preliminary fashion and indicate the direction of further investigation. That account draws primarily on the "performative theory of utterance." What has been said thus far concerns the form or appearance of criticism; the theory of performatives may serve to locate that appearance within a

77

conceptual framework. The criteria defining the class of critical judgments are provided for in that theory.

The concept of performative utterance was originally introduced by J. L. Austin as an emendation of the cognitive-emotive dichotomy of linguistic usage that had been formulated in certain earlier theories of utterance.[15] Austin hoped by the concept to take account of an apparently small group of utterances like "I apologize" or "Passengers are requested to fasten their seat belts," which have the peculiar property of performing the action they mention, not of describing it or exclaiming about it, which were the principal linguistic functions acknowledged in the dichotomy against which he reacted. In analyzing the structure of performatives, however, Austin's attention was drawn to the fact that a surprisingly large number of utterances seemed to fit within the boundaries of the new class, if to its more obvious conditions a distinction was added between explicit performatives, like the examples cited, and primary performatives, such as, "Forward, march!" in which a performative prefix for the utterance (e.g., "I order you to . . .") was implied. With the latter expansion, the concept of performatives verges on a general theory of utterance; there are few utterances, if any, to which such prefixes cannot be attached. Austin was himself reluctant to proceed in this direction; but the account here takes the possibility seriously, suggesting that the performative theory *could* yield a general account of utterance. I shall attempt, in any event, to show the effectiveness of that theory in accounting for the formal character ascribed here to critical judgment.

Performative utterances characteristically are required to satisfy two principal conditions: (a) that the primary force of the utterance be not descriptive or hortatory, but active; that is, that the utterance should itself constitute the action designated by it; (b) that the action comprised by the utterance be in accord with a pertinent set of conventions. What these conditions amount to will be evident with respect to the utterance, "I order you to march forward." The utterance is the order, but it functions as an order only if a sergeant gives the order to a corporal and not the other way around. Conventions such as this one vary with the action taken. We must see, then, what these would be for critical judgment, although it is important first to determine in what sense critical judgment is performative at all.

The key to this identification resides in that factor of reflective judgment according to which reflective judgment goes beyond any of the ostensibly syntactic elements of the work. The object disclosed by reflective judgment is not simply the object as detached, viewed impersonally and through lenses which have been independently focused; it is rather the object as the critic, by his lights, contrives or shapes it and then offers it as an object of perception to his audience. He accomplishes the presentation by way of the work of criticism, by *its* statements. Those statements are not simply descriptive, for, as we have seen, the underlying process of reflective judgment is not itself simply descriptive; it projects a pattern or order which is not realized prior to the judgment. The critic's statements, I contend, thus answer to the conditions of performatory utterance in the sense that each such statement has a tacit or primary prefix addressed to the reader: "I [the critic] show you that the work is (or means or implies) such-and-such." Or, put slightly differently, in a variation on ritualistic performative: "I [the critic] present to you [my reader] the work as . . . ."

Other implied prefixes might be supplied for critical judgments, and no doubt a variety is necessary to account for the shades of critical presentation. What any of the variations must include, however, is the sense of presentation or exhibition, a sense which is consummated in the properties or qualities to which such prefixes are the introduction. The critic's statements, if they are felicitous, disclose what he sees; and that disclosure is effected for the viewer by way of the statements themselves as they discriminate referents for his attention.

The specific conventions which critical judgment observes (the second of the conditions cited above) may be formulated in a number of ways; with one exception, they are at any rate not crucial to the present discussion. One might stipulate, for example, that the object at the focus of the critic's judgment must exist in some physical, nonaesthetic mode; that the critic should have had some experience of it; and that he should be governed by no ulterior, noncritical interest in the verdict he formulates, such as a commission from the sale of a painting. A critical judgment wanting in such respects will not be felicitous, although it might well be felicitous as an instance of another type of judgment. This list, again, is not intended as exhaustive or exclusive; the formal argument requires only the acknowledgment that such conditions pertain and must be satisfied for critical judgment to be felicitous.

The single exception to this variable list of the relevant conventions is a feature which applies only to some performatives but which is essential to critical judgment—what may be designated as a consequent convention. A wager, in Austin's example, is not fully a wager until a second party to the transaction, the party challenged to bet, says "Done." The statement "I made a bet with Smith, but Smith refused to bet" would be nonsensical. The account of reflective judgment suggests analogously that the felicity of critical judgments is also tied to the assent of an audience in terms of consequent conditions, that the critical judgment will not be consummated until the critic's audience responds (and means) "agreed" or, more specifically, "seen" to the statements of the critic. Critical judgments do not become felicitous through the critic's verbal expression alone; they only may come to be felicitous. If the critic intends to "show" some aspect or meaning to his audience, the aspect or meaning he articulates is part of a felicitous critical judgment only when his audience acknowledges it. *For otherwise it would not have been "shown."* The critic, on these terms, not only performs, but, like artists or actors, depends on the reception given his performance. What he does logically presupposes a response—not *to* that which he does (as though that were somehow autonomous), but in order that it may be done at all.

This translation of reflective judgment into terms of the performative theory faces a number of substantial objections; it may seem to have sharpened the problematic features in the account of reflective judgment. Can we argue seriously that what the varieties of criticism present would not exist without a response to the judgment itself? Surely, one might object, the contriteness of which Wittkower speaks, even granting that it is not a "given" gesture of the Bernini sculpture, has some independence of the judgment which articulates it. But an answer is latent in the objection itself. Such features may seem finally to win some independence of the judgment, but with independence there is no middle ground: the features must be either independent or not, and the analysis of reflective judgment is clear in its claim that they are not. They may be grounded in syntactic elements, but, finally, they escape the constraints of those elements; indeed, as I have argued, they serve the latter as a basis, not the other way round.

What then becomes of the object outside the critical context or judgment, the object *qua* object? It will be evident that for all the patent difficulties implied in such a contention, the thesis I have argued would render such a question virtually unintelligible. Its gloss on the question would be "What is the object of art when it is undisclosed or unknown?" And to that, it seems, the only judicious answer must be that the object of art is then indeed unknown. Reflective judgment is not a device used by the critic only to communicate to his audience: it is, even before that, the means by which the critic himself grasps the work; and it is, still prior to *that*, the means by which the object of art exists as art.

This conclusion may appear, if not to beg the question of the art work's status, at least to open itself to a number of pressing subordinate objections. It will be noted, for one, that the judgments of criticism as performative become a function not only of the critic but also of his reader, and it may be further argued that the role of the critic is not, as a matter of fact, determined by the agreement commanded by a particular judgment or work of criticism. It seems quite arbitrary to claim, as is apparently implied in the performative theory, that the acknowledgment of a single reader of the critical judgment should suffice to establish the difference between criticism and noncriticism. But imagine a critical work in which the judgments commanded no assent at all. Is it only an extraordinarily perverse or ingenious piece of criticism? The statements which that critic makes resemble the statements of other writers whose judgments have some force. But if we are to preserve a place for bad critics (and surely we ought to), we must be able to distinguish them from good critics and even more importantly from noncritics; it is an obvious line that can be drawn between criticism and noncriticism at the point where a writer who may have met the other conditions of criticism fails to enable anyone to see what it is that he is showing. The showing, the implied prefix of critical judgment, implies a taking as well as a giving; it makes little sense to speak of something as shown but not seen.

A more cogent version of the same objection might be taken to dispute the implication that since the minimal assent of a single observer establishes critical judgment as felicitous, beyond that point all critical judgments, even those which contradict each other, seem to exert the same force; or as a variation on this objection that on the theory presented, the more felicitous judgment of two conflicting ones will be the one which commands the largest assent in terms of the extent of an audience. In a minimal sense the former of these objections is undeniable: all criticism is equal insofar as it is criticism. This would be persuasive as an objection, however, only if no degrees of cogency or felicity qualified individual judgments; and nothing said so far implies that consequence. The second implication cited indicates an alternative to the grounds of the objection: in some sense of the "extent" of agreement, extent itself provides a standard by which the felicity of critical judgment may be measured. The sense in which this holds will be clarified through a view of the conditions which affect that extent.

The most important of these conditions is what might be called the "test of coherence." The cogency of a particular critical judgment, for the reader of criticism no less than for the critic, is determined in part by its relations to other judgments. So far as it is inconsistent with other critical or noncritical judgments, the judgment awaits a decision on the conflicting claims. *Hamlet*, for example, could be interpreted as a bedroom comedy but only at the expense of numerous syntactic and reflective judgments which are otherwise held to apply to *Hamlet* and, beyond it, to other common examples of bedroom comedy and tragedy. The critic who values Rod McKuen as a great poet must face the question of what value he will place on Keats. Admittedly, he may persist and in effect construct a world of critical discourse in which Keats is a lesser poet than McKuen; he may reach this qualitative conclusion even on the basis of a painstaking derivation and comparison of the reflective judgments which apply; and he may find or create an audience which follows him. Such incongruities may arise in any instance of reflective judgment; the expectation with which we await the resolution of such conflict is no more than that. We may argue that in the long run, disagreement in the ranking of Keats and McKuen will be resolved, that with a conscientious effort on all sides the issue will be settled. And it is true enough that the consensus actually reached in the assessment of works of art is much more notable a feature in the history of criticism than is disagreement. One simply does not find critical claims for the triviality of Dostoyevsky's conception of evil or for Manet's moral perversity, no matter what the initial critical response to their work was. If what I have said about the persuasive character of critical judgment holds, such unanimity is due as much to the standards derived in the works of Dostoyevsky or Manet as to any independent source; but the fact of the consensus is striking nonetheless.

In some cases, however, even the winnowing process of history, as it pushes and is pulled by criticism, has not sufficed and probably will not. In certain instances disagreement persists not because of any failing in the audience, but because of intentional or unintentional ambiguity in the aesthetic object. In other cases, disagreement may reflect systematic faults in instruments of criticism. Few viewers of art, for example, will deny the relevance to their view of an awareness of art's social context; but the pertinence of this factor does not imply that others must be excluded, others such as the psychological or religious contexts. At the point at which such exclusion is required, the test of coherence is decisive: the Marxist who regards the work of art exclusively as a mirror of the social interests of the individual artist must be prepared to defend that view for any case within the arts (no easy matter, as Marx himself found with one of his favorite authors, Balzac) as well as for its more general esteem of Marxism as a philosophical account.

Moreover, there are cases in which differences in interpretation do not conflict but represent complementary and therefore noncontradictory emphases. A variety of nonexclusive reflective concepts may fruitfully apply to any critical object; they no more contradict each other than to see the duck-rabbit cartoon as a duck contradicts the seeing of it as a rabbit. Thus, that it is illuminating to read *Hamlet* in the light of psychoanalytic principles hardly in itself implies that other principles are irrelevant, as there need be no stipulation by psychoanalysis in general that its conclusions exhaust the extent of the explanations of human action. It is often clear that only as one form of analysis is supplemented by others do we gain a full sense of the possibilities sponsored by the object.

The question persists beyond these considerations, however, of what resolution is possible for conflicting critical judgments in cases where none of the solutions cited work—for example, where the duck-rabbit is seen as neither duck nor rabbit, but elephant; where pushpin is taken to be quite as good as poetry, where it is insisted that *Hamlet* is a rollicking bedroom farce. It may concede the perplexity too easily; there seems to be no theoretical alternative in such extremity, however, except to acknowledge that the critics responsible for those judgments and the audiences whom they win over have created and inhabit worlds of their own, perhaps improbable ones, ones which are likely to prove inconsistent with respect to important aspects of experience, but which at any rate cannot be denied as possible. The universes of discourse articulated on this very large scale are not so much contradictory as exclusive of each other. The elements involved in each one are sufficiently comprehensive that they may reasonably be assumed to be the only standard by which a comparison with other hypotheses or judgments can be made; thus other, conflicting judgments lose out.

This consequence of incommensurability poses the most serious qualification on the measurement of the felicity of critical judgment by the extent or degree of concurrence. In the cases of deepest or sharpest disagreement, the very possibility of comparative measurement or assessment is foreclosed: critics and viewers on either side are not only a critical judgment apart, but, literally, are worlds apart. They disagree not about a single object or aspect, but about a large set of objects and aspects, approaching the point where the term disagreement itself is only a metaphor. Furthermore, there is no ground for arguing that such situations cannot arise, if only because they have arisen. *Hamlet* may indeed be an "artistic failure," as Eliot claimed and as some of his readers have been persuaded; and finally there is no way of proving or disproving this claim for the readers of *Hamlet* who regard it as a triumph. Not because there is no disputing about taste, but because after critics have disputed all that there is to dispute, the question of what an audience sees in a given work of art may remain open. This conclusion can come as no surprise to the reader who has followed the argument so far. For if reflective judgment indeed goes beyond the syntactic elements of the object of art as the critic or viewer contrives it, one can hardly expect a consensus, even on the largest issues. We shall later see how this limitation on criticism which places criticism, at some point, "beyond dispute" is rooted in the ontological openness of art itself. That history or conscience will eventually settle such differences may commend itself as an article of faith, but it can be no more than that. Critical judgment, quite simply, has no touchstone.

Despite the possibility of such large and irreconcilable critical discrepancies, however, the fact remains that substantial controls can be invoked before they arise, that the greatest number of such differences are either marginal or will be settled in a much shorter run, where inconsistency and inadequacy may be made evident. It may be overly rationalistic to argue that, granting the possibility of innovation, human differences as regards totalities of experience tend to disappear. But it is a matter of fact that, pushed onto the large scale of human nature, such differences diminish; and there, finally—again, in the critic's audience—resides whatever prospect there is for the reconciliation of critical disagreement. It is almost certainly not the case—on the basis of experience alone—that *Hamlet* both is and is not a bedroom farce, and we do not have to rely on the initial *obiter dicta* of criticism as the court before which the case must be argued. The bare claims themselves count only for single moments; but they imply and are themselves tied to a large network of judgments and forms of sensibility; and before the specific claims of conflicting reflective judgments can be judged for adequacy, we must have also followed them into these related networks. That complexity, if it pertains at all, will reduce the initial divergence; criticism is in its turn open there to judgment. There is nothing invidious in the requirement that the critical process be coherent as well as inventive.

Thus, even at the last point, where we acknowledge that the process of criticism in disclosing an object is a variable and human project, the hope of controls persists. Like any single moment of vision, criticism will not exhaust the sources of experience; neither (tautologously) does it operate independently of them. Its commitment is set within the limits of aesthetic object and the powers of the percipient; indefinite as those limits are, they nonetheless offer a dialectical control for and upon the critics of the critic—his audience—who either do or do not see what the critic asserts to be present. There is, after all, an outline to the object encountered, and there is, after all, an audience which shares certain impulses and powers. The fact that the critic has to pick himself and his audience up by the bootstraps in order to get beyond the undiscriminated elements with which they all begin means that he has at least those grounds to move from and as an end to reckon with.[16] It is tautologous to say that the range of criticism is limited by the nature of the critic and thus by the nature he shares with or creates for his audience. But if this is tautologous, it is a self-contradiction to deny it and to maintain either that the range of critical judgment is more open or more diffuse than experience as a whole, or so closed that we must accept it arbitrarily as the critic—*any* critic—finds it. The formidable risks which remain are but the other side of the possibilities engendered by a creative and persuasive critical imagination, and, indeed, by art itself.

Several issues postponed at earlier stages of this chapter remain to be mentioned, if only to postpone certain of them again. One question concerned the ability of the performative theory of utterance to distinguish the class of critical judgments from other types of utterance. Unless that distinction can be drawn, especially with reference to the distinctive features of critical judgment (for example, its persuasive character), the performative analysis of critical judgment as a whole can have little force.

It is not possible to attempt a typology of linguistic performance here. Some indication can be given, nonetheless, of method—of how the types can be discriminated. Two principal variables might guide this discrimination: the formal structure of the judgment to be categorized and the end which it serves. With respect to the former: it has been suggested that critical judgment involves a consequent condition. One means of categorizing judgments may then be in terms of the presence or absence of such a condition. A second, probably more substantial categorical aspect may be referred to the anterior conditions of the judgment. For example, interest in personal gain may be an admissible, even a necessary, condition of judgments reflecting personal desires or likes; but there is good reason why such interest should be absent from legal verdicts. The problem is to work out a set of categories, in terms of personal interest or whatever, which apply generally and which will then serve as a classificatory device for lines drawn among the varieties of judgment.

The second, more fundamental, parameter referred to is that of selecting, isolating, and characterizing the functioning of the judgments. The goal here, a central one for grasping individual types of judgment or the role of judgment as such, is to

87

discriminate among the various ends which judgments serve. There seems to be a significant variety in those uses in the actions which judgment serves. To conceive of judgment as characteristically performative, a doing, is to presume on the possibility of drawing lines among the different kinds of things which are done.

Of those questions previously deferred, a second concerns the evidence on which the account of critical judgment has been based: whether critical judgment characteristically is persuasive and whether, as such, it fits the conditions cited of a type of performative utterance. I have not claimed that the distinctions drawn here provide the only possible means of categorizing critical judgment, but rather that, however the lines are drawn, the evidence on which the distinctions are based must be taken into account. That evidence is, quite simply, critical practice. The test of what is asserted in this allocation to categories is easily formalized: whether extraneous or irrelevant items of evidence have been included, and whether other forms or instances of criticism have been ignored; whether the account itself is consistent; and, what yet remains to be seen, how fruitful are the categories which have been applied for the understanding of art as art and not simply as critical object. Such criteria may be difficult to apply, but *what* they are is evident.

Criticism: The "Final Cause." The question of the end, the "final cause" of criticism, has gone unmentioned in the preceding comments; but both the question and an answer to it are implicit. In discussing the process of criticism, I have held that its immediate function is to communicate to his audience the critic's articulation of aspects which belong to an object only in a highly attenuated sense—in effect, to get the audience to see not what is there but what may be, what finally, by its own imperatives, should be construed there. The evidence of criticism suggests that the end of this process is not persuasion itself. Certain critics, of course, may have that end as a motive, and any given audience may wish to be persuaded. But it is unlikely (even in these events and certainly as a general rule) that the object of persuasion, what the critic's reader is to be persuaded of, should be a matter of indifference.

This quality of the object which is at stake in the process of criticism suggests an obvious, though still problematic, end for criticism. If the critic has designs on the perception of aspects of the work of art, then the end of criticism should be the convergence of criticism on art itself. For it is art which, if anything is, is the object of criticism. The perception to which the critic invites his audience is what he has been offered by art; insofar as he is successful, his audience will realize that fact as they penetrate what had been opaque, as they dispel earlier perplexities by confronting the art work more resourcefully—in short, as they see the work. The critic, in this regard, is no more than a member of the audience of art, and to inquire about the final end of criticism, it turns out, is to inquire about the end of art.

This connection was foreshadowed in the opening lines of this essay as the basically "heteronomous" character of critical judgment. Acknowledgment of this extrinsic end for criticism is, however, not to denigrate criticism or to consign it to a rarefied domain of specialization or technology. To identify something as the means to an end is not to choose between them. It is clear—and will in later chapters be made clearer—that the critical process characterized here, far from being the preserve of some single group of art's viewers, is practiced by them all. Special expertise may be evident in some applications of critical perception but there is some expertise in all of them. Criticism as an act is not the special occupation of a small group of experts; those experts, like their audience, are first and finally viewers of art.

The questions remaining from this analysis may seem as large as the ones answered by it. In directing philosophical inquiry through criticism to art, we begin to ask about moments of experience rather than about the customs of language. Such moments encompass extra-linguistic as well as linguistic elements. They point to the overarching questions which mark the analysis of human nature—what it is in man which leads him to the criticism, and beyond or prior to that, to the appreciation of art; and, on another side, what the structure is of the objects which foster those activities. More immediately, the question persists of the character of the reflective basis of critical judgment and (on the basis of what has just been said) of art itself. Even if everything asserted so far were granted, we should not yet have accounted for the drawing power of the reflective judgments which have art as their object. For surely that power, if reflective judgment no more than approximates its presentation here, is preeminent among the features of art. What has been formulated so far is a schema, not an explanation. Chapter 3 completes the schema with an account of the denotative force of reflective judgment; with that, the work of explanation begins.

A final comment about what has been asserted to be the open texture of critical judgment is needed. This openness can apply to criticism only if it first and more fundamentally characterizes the object of criticism, a fact which implies the probability of ambivalence, of construction and emendation, in the work of art as well as in the judgment of criticism. But surely this implication no more conflicts with the experience of art than it does with respect to the act of criticism. The challenge of both art and criticism is little different from that which we encounter in simply opening our eyes—the act in which criticism begins. The end of that act and of critical judgment bear an important resemblance: without them we do not see. The check, furthermore, on aberrant criticism is identical with that on aberrant perception; not from seeing less but from seeing more do we arrive at a position to criticize distortions or to expand the grasp of understanding. There is no guarantee that a particular moment in the critical process will illuminate the work of art any more than the viewer knows beforehand what, in first opening his eyes, he will see. The end at which he will arrive if he does not accept the risk, however, is certain; and the critical enterprise, attending to art, thus finds its justification there, in the experience which, as the viewer comes to know, art offers.

The Work in Process

The critic, first and last, is a viewer of art (if not the view itself). As he imposes ideological principle or personal affect, he may succeed as theoretician or poet; but the art work will elude him. He should have free vision and a strong imagination: the legends of the profession. And not only, of course, professionally. We know, from the intentions of Everyman, as he looks if not as he says, that attending to art, he too aspires to the condition of critic; so his critics can tell. Not that he is always apt; it is the technology of criticism rather than its perfections which is the currency of vision.

It has been objected that criticism is written (and read) in the Winter of Hindsight, that it intellectualizes on what art's lovers know as an affair of the heart. "The more profound the abstraction, the shallower the touch of reality"—so the war against critical vice, with small intimation of critical virtue. But criticism, though written in hindsight, is founded and completed in the present. And if it appears to be discursive (in the fashion of judgment), one must, to assert that this is irrelevant, have shown art as impervious. Criticism may be abused, but not only by the critic. This leaves it the breadth of its uses. We have always before us the question of how the eye—if it wanted to—would see without an apparatus; that is, without the eye. Resort to immediacy may come at last, as no doubt it comes first; but there is a distance to be traveled in between.

Reflective judgment, the medium of criticism, is thus contrived not exclusively by the critic as expositor, but by the viewer as viewer. Its form reflects the encounter with art; to follow the course of its judgment then, not surprisingly, is to be driven to art. The characteristics imposing on reflective judgment are the energy and the inventiveness of its process and the peculiar generality of its conclusions. Its terms and intentions are rooted in a measure of experience; but they are not specified there, as we know from the many times when we mistakenly substitute for them historical description, artistic autobiography, or simply the reservoir of free association. Finally, it is the specific mark of an experience, like the expressive line in a face, that is at stake. The judgment of appreciation may start from, but goes well beyond, the bounds of either the viewer or the object alone.

A question then comes to light concerning the process of the judgment, of the resolve of its activity. On the surface the moments of art may seem, even through the dark glass of criticism, innocent enough; as we follow the expansions of those moments, we often find ourselves wanting to stop as we had hoped to begin, with the thing itself. Yet the evidence persists, pointed by the vectors of criticism, of a form of implication moving from the single line between the object and the viewer's response to a reach beyond either the object's physical limits or the viewer's private self: this we know even from the existence of reflective judgment. What this leaves, aside from the experience, is a question for aesthetic inquiry which is directed towards an existence for art, a way of being and intelligibility—a place which reflection sets for it which, by the process of reflection, extends beyond the place set.

Common to the modes of criticism as they converge on the point of reflective judgment is the proposal of an object sought, an object, now, not as inert, but intentionally, as goal. The terms in which goals are conceived are as various as goals or their seekers, and we are left with the leeway of a choice. But even with decisions, there are conventions to be acknowledged, proprieties to be observed, a form. What we know of art, whether by knowing art or only by following the judgments on it, is its expansiveness, the circumference to which, on sight, it seems to grow. To look hard at a work of art may also be to look around it and even through it. But more compellingly still, it is to look in to it.

Perhaps no object gives itself away easily or neatly but, if this is generally so, then art's objects in particular do it less than others. And since this is so, we expect to see something more than a surface. Thus, the recurrence of reflective judgment.

The encounter with art will not be inert, but, we may hope, translucent—the encounter itself supplying the light. And what translucence requires in the understanding is an idiom for describing passage or evocation.

The painter's products stand before us as though they were alive, but if you question them, they maintain a most majestic silence. It is the same with written words; they seem intelligent, but if you ask them anything about what they say, from a desire to be instructed, they go on telling you just the same thing forever.

Plato, *Phaedrus*

The arrow points only in the application which the living being makes of it.

Wittgenstein, *Philosophical Investigations*

3

Denotation
and Aesthetic Inference

The categories introduced in the account of criticism in chapter 2 may seem peripheral to the status of the work of art itself; but the question to which they point for aesthetic inquiry—what must exist as art if the critical judgments of art exist—is straightforward. The examples cited of reflective judgment differ in certain respects; but beyond their suggestion of the role of reflective judgment in criticism, they testify in common to an experience and finally to an object. The principal question thus posed by the discussion is what those are: what is it that reflective judgment intends, what does the judgment come to?

This question, I suggest, may be approached by way of that feature of reflective judgment of the three indicated which has not yet been discussed: its denotative status. The issues raised in this connection have been, it will be recognized, at stake in the long-standing discussion of cognition or truth in art (although not only there): if art denotes, then to comprehend the structure of art is to have discerned something about its cognitive force. The attempt here to face the question of the denotative status of reflective judgment is thus related to that broader discussion. This is one way, and for all its complication, a fruitful one, of opening up the further question of what the end of art is.

A Conceptual Background. The issue of the cognitive status of art has traditionally generated more heat than light, and, in this respect at least, contemporary philosophical thought has been devoted to its past. The phenomenon is the more notable because of the attentiveness of both classical and modern philosophy to the analysis of knowledge and truth. The lag in relating the theory of knowledge to the theory of art is undoubtedly not without its own significance for the historiography of philosophy. Whatever the explanation, the fact remains that the categories in terms of which the relation between art and knowledge has been formulated as a philosophical issue have been almost without exception adequate only to one or the other side of the relation. Given this initial limitation, little might have been expected beyond it.

One element in this failure has been a confusion of the cognitive status of the work of art and of the spectator's knowledge or beliefs in his appreciation of the work. The difference between those facets of the aesthetic moment seems obvious enough, even if there are also points at which they touch. To analyze its cognitive status is to consider whether and how a work of art serves as a source of knowledge—in the terms to be taken up here, how it denotes; the second question, of the connection between art and belief, is a question of how the truth or falsity of art's cognitive claims affects or should affect the experience of which the work of art is the focus. The latter question thus assumes an affirmative answer to the former.

The two questions have, nonetheless, been conflated. A notable instance of this conflation and of the confusion which must follow it figures in the most common rendering of Plato's theory of art,[1] which finds in Plato's reflections on art, especially as they appear in the *Republic*, the thesis that art by its nature corrupts, leading its audience away from the practice of reason. Because of this, the work of the artist must in some of its varieties be excluded from the ideal polity; always it must be rigorously censored. Persuasion and emotional appeal can be justified in that polity only in the interest of truth, and that interest itself plays a slight, often perverse, role in the artist's creations.

According to this reading, the onus of Plato's criticism is on art itself; and it is here that the confusion alluded to seems to have taken hold. For although there is no doubt that Plato impugns *some* conception of art in books 2, 3, and 10 in the *Republic*, the occasion of his criticism and of his irony (related to the occasion and irony of the *Republic* as a whole) is what Plato has found to be a popular attitude, surely that of members of the Athenian audience toward art; for example, as they understand Homer's references to the gods as an historical account and thus as a guide for conduct. The conception of art underlying this attitude ascribes cognitive status to the objects of art, but it is a status which results from a mistaken conception which identifies poetic description as history or gospel. Plato criticizes this confusion in the objects of knowledge; but his objection is directed not against a defect in art so much as it is against the failure of the viewers of art to refine their criteria of belief and of art. His attack, in fact, does little to illuminate the question of the cognitive status of art itself (Plato's position on that issue, although related to these other objections, must be viewed through his epistemology, for example, in the *Republic*, books 6 and 7, and in the writings specifically about beauty, as in the *Symposium*, the *Phaedrus* and the *Philebus*.) The criticism of art in the *Republic* and in the *Ion* is, on these terms, an attack on an audience of art, on the expectations which they bring to it and the criteria by which they judge it; to miss this systematic distinction is probably also to misconstrue Plato's theory of art and even his epistemology. Certainly it reflects a failure to isolate the question of the cognitive status of art.

A second, more general, historical reference indicates the tendency of our present discussion. That the relation between art and knowledge has been a recurrent issue in the recent philosophical literature should not obscure the fact that this represents a revision, or more precisely a revival, in the program of aesthetic inquiry. For Greek thought, in Plato, Aristotle, the Stoics, the issue of the cognitive status of art was live and important; we find a similar, in some ways more specific, attentiveness in the recent Hegelian tradition, in such writers as Cassirer, Dewey, and Lukacs and in the phenomenological accounts of Heidegger, Ingarden, Dufrenne, and Hofstadter. The differences among such figures notwithstanding, their accounts of the project of art share a common thesis which asserts the possibility of integrating aesthetic and cognitive implication, of characterizing them as aspects of a single, more fundamental mode in the articulation of experience.

In Kant's work, however, which stands between the fore-named historical parallels as the watershed of modern aesthetic theory, the very question of the connection between beauty or aesthetic experience and knowledge is disputed. The background of this denial is the background to Kant's larger dissent from the "dogmatism" of his predecessors, one tenet of which, originally applied to aesthetics by Baumgarten, was the homogeneity of judgment—aesthetic judgment together with the others. Kant's opposition to that drive for unity was largely influenced, with respect to aesthetic theory, by British empiricism, specifically the work of such authors as Burke and Hume, for whom a distinction between the activities of taste and reason was fundamental. From such origins, Kant comes to rest his aesthetics on the leading question of how the judgment of taste, as distinct from cognitive judgment, for one, can be accounted for. The latter distinction is adopted as a premise to his aesthetic system; and the intent and consequences of this program, as Kant formulated it, have reappeared periodically, sometimes independently, more often under the weight of his influence, in such idioms as the analysis of Form or of Aesthetic Pleasure or of Aesthetic Surface—each or all regarded as autonomous objects of aesthetic inquiry.

The revival of interest in the traditional terms of the problem of art's truth followed principally from a reaction against this (among others) of Kant's distinctions.[2] Hegel, the largest figure in this reaction, saw in the appearances of beauty a "semblance" of universal reason; art, itself a moment in an encompassing process, was then necessarily related to the other moments of that process. Attempts to elaborate on this expansion by Hegel of the province of reason provided a recurrent philosophical theme for the nineteenth century; the detail of their concern with art on the part of the twentieth-century writers mentioned above (in many other ways quite different), is historically comprehensible only in light of that common source.

For all the objections to which the aesthetic theories incorporating that theme are liable, a promise emerges in their design of a more adequate account of the facts of aesthetic experience than that supplied by the formalist tradition against which they react; this, at all events, is the supposition underlying the general thesis argued here.

A last prefatory comment: although the title of this chapter speaks of aesthetic inference, I refer initially for evidence and example to literature. This is a tactical move influenced by the medium of literature, however, not a limitation on the range of aesthetic inference. The various arts converge at certain crucial points; I hope to show that analysis of the denotative status of literature, as that status is attested in the propositional form of reflective judgment, provides a model by which the cognitive status of the other arts can be estimated as well.

Aesthetic Denotation—The Prima Facie Evidence. The two accounts of the cognitive status of literary works of art which serve here as introduction agree on at least one thesis—that the connection between literary works of art and truth is no more (and probably less) than tenuous. They suggest, as an implication of Russell's Theory of Definite Descriptions, that the statements of literature are for the largest part false; or, in terms of I. A. Richards's "emotive-cognitive" distinction, that literary discourse does not meet the criteria for determining that a statement is either true or false, and thus that judgments which impose such criteria are irrelevant. These accounts were modified by their authors after their initial formulation; if only as a contrast to the thesis argued here, however, it is useful to examine them in their original form.

Russell, in his classic essay "On Denoting," examines a group of statements which seem clear and intelligible in their linguistic structure, but which are distinctive in that they cite nonexistent entities, for example, "Pegasus" or "the present King of France." [3] The truth status of statements that incorporate such terms is problematic; they can hardly be accounted true, but neither do they seem to be false in the manner of ordinary

99

contrary-to-fact descriptions. Their assessment must turn on the denotative force of the terms, more specifically on the difference between those terms and other terms about whose denotation there is little question. Rejecting Meinong's schema of modes or levels of reality that reflect the differences among such references, Russell introduces a conception of definite descriptions according to which statements like "The present King of France is bald" or "The present King of France is not bald" are isomorphic to statements made concerning an actual king. This conclusion follows, Russell suggests, if we take all particular assertions to affirm the existence of a subject; so, for example, the first of the statements mentioned can be formulated as "There is a being who is King of France and who is bald," a proposition which we know to be false in the same way that we know the statement "France is thirty miles wide" to be false. We are enabled by this method, Russell suggests, to account for the denotative status of terms in all propositions, including those with such "nonexistent" referents as the "round square," or (the case most pertinent here) "Hamlet"; and this is accomplished without the encumbrance of an hierarchy of levels or types of reality.

The question of the adequacy of this general account of denotation is less to the immediate point than are its implications for the denotative force of literature. It follows from Russell's position, as a number of writers pointed out in the discussion which enlarged on it,[4] that since statements in literary works would be open to translation as definite descriptions, those statements turn out by and large to be false; and that the truth status of the works in which they appear must then take account of this. As an illustration, the statements in *Pickwick Papers* describing Mr. Pickwick's activities are—since Mr. Pickwick, on Russell's account, existed in not even a Pickwickian sense—false; to the extent that such statements comprise the book's contents, assessment of the truth status of the novel as a whole will be similarly determined.

This analysis was not calculated, however, either in its method or conclusions, to end a discussion with a history as involuted as that of the cognitive status of art. One important reaction against it was that of I. A. Richards, whose "defense" of literature points a classic lesson of the risk of throwing out the bath water while the baby is still in the tub.[5] Linguistic utterances which are true or false, Richards argues, constitute but one type of utterance. Those utterances are true or false insofar as they represent or misrepresent actual states of affairs. But not all utterances serve the same function; and it is a mistake to assess the statements of literature as cognitive, and thus, as on Russell's theory, usually as false, since it is not their function to denote or to describe at all. They represent rather an emotive or noncognitive use of language, designed to express an author's feelings or to evoke an emotive response from his audience. They belong not to the universe of scientific discourse with its concern for what really exists or not, but to that of the language of feeling; as such they are neither true nor false. They are not actually statements at all, but rather, in Richards's term, "pseudo-statements." We may then evaluate them by criteria of emotional intensity or of the power of evocation but hardly in terms of the adequacy of representation or denotation to which they make no claim.

The advantage gained by dissociating literary works of art from cognitive assertion as against regarding them as false is problematic, even if the position were to be argued consistently; and criticism directed at the consistency of Richards's thesis seems conclusive.[6] Yet the difference between the accounts of Richards and Russell is instructive in one respect. To abstract from Richards's argument is to recognize a corollary thesis that it is an error of method and, finally, of substance to focus analysis of the denotative status of literary statements on their literal force. Those statements assuredly can be assessed independently and out of their literary context, by strict empirical or any other criteria of verification. But given the fact of their appearance in a literary context, it is unlikely that this extraneous procedure will accurately represent what the statements in that context assert, let alone determine adequately what their truth status is. Before the assertions or implications attributed to the work of art can be tested for truth or falsity, in other words, we must identify what the work in fact asserts or implies; and it should not be assumed, according to Richards, that the work as art is comprised exclusively, if at all, of its ostensive statements and denotative terms. To assume this is to take for granted that the denotation of a term and of the units of which it is part are fixed independently of their contextual function. That may be the case, but it certainly does not go without saying.

This principle of Richards's analysis gains support from the *reductio* argument which follows its denial, a fact of which Richards obviously is aware. If we examine literary statements out of their literary context, assessing them by criteria borrowed from the practice of scientific or practical discourse, many of them turn out to be false. If, to extend that process, we construe an individual work of literature as a network of conjunctive statements (for instance, " 'It's a vile attempt to extort money,' said Mr. Pickwick [and] 'I hope it is,' said Wardle, with a short, dry cough."), then the work which contains even a single false statement is false not only to that extent but as a whole. This assessment, however, which would apply to virtually every work of literature is prima facie inadequate. Even if we admit the difficulty of specifying the claims which are affirmed in literary works of art, the fact remains that an important point of relevance for some of them seems a profundity of thought which could hardly weigh so heavily if the assertions themselves were simply and flatly false. One need not commit oneself to any particular theory of truth or of beauty, or of their equation either, to acknowledge the force with which certain works of literature engage the reader's concern with certain real aspects of the world and how they might yet be. That concern is not academic; and it could not obtain, one supposes, unless its grounds were located in the work itself—unless the work articulated certain live possibilities of experience.

Admittedly, this thesis finds in falsity the connotation of triviality; and different falsehoods are open to that charge in varying degrees. No less obviously, not everything which is true is by that fact important or profound.[7] Nor does it follow from what has been said that the truth of literature in itself gives literature its power. But these qualifications, individually or together, do not controvert the prima facie evidence. To be sure, that evidence is not *proof* that the work of art has denotative force of an order different from that attributed to it by Russell—or any denotative force at all. It serves, however, as a significant indicator for the account of denotation begun in chapter 2 in connection with reflective judgment. More generally, it defines a factor for which any account of the relation between art and knowledge must make provision even if it chooses a different idiom than that of denotation by which to do so.

This same evidence, it should be noted, is finally skewed by Richards himself when he labels the pseudo-statements of literature as emotive. The artist and his work are thus set aside from the world of discursive knowledge, a distinction which, like the confusion of categories in Russell's account of literary statement, ends contrary to facts which we do not have to go far to find. When Burns writes "My luv's like a red, red rose," for example, we surely misappropriate the line if we take it to be only an expression of his feeling (if we could even agree on what this last phrase means), implying nothing about the character of his "luv." The line's expressive character notwithstanding, the poet seems also to represent objects or qualities which his reader is expected to recognize and in terms of which he can—and, if he is to understand it, must—appreciate the line's force. Not all "luvs" *are* like roses; the differences among them are not exclusively, perhaps not even primarily, emotive.

The result is, then, that the principle which animates his criticism initially, that the denotative force of literary discourse is not to be found in its literal statements, is eventually undercut in Richards's conclusion that it has no denotative force whatever. The implications of that conclusion suggest the need for a course of analysis that would stop short of its extremity without yet denying the first principle. It would be useful, in other words, to be able to distinguish in the statements of literature (and, as I shall attempt to show, in the data of art in general) between an ostensive and an inferred denotation, between the literal and aesthetic force of statements. Such an alternative, I have suggested, would have the weight of prima facie evidence on its side; it must show beyond this that such evidence is worth adhering to, that it makes sense in the context of a general theory of meaning. In the forthcoming discussion I attempt to see how this implicit denotation works in practice and then to analyze it more formally. I shall argue, specifically, that works of art are denotative; that their denotation is made explicit through a process of aesthetic inference which demonstrates by its relevance the irrelevance of the literal denotation of the work's individual elements; and that what is denoted is qualified, in effect bracketed, by a framework of generality with respect to temporal and spatial location. The last condition sponsors a mode of experience that acquires aesthetic force as the framework of generality intentionally engages the individual observer. The argument on this last point, continued here from the preceding discussion, extends also to chapters 4 and 5.

Aesthetic Inference. The means by which the work of art is realized in reflective judgment can be formulated in terms of the concept of aesthetic inference—a process, I shall argue, which is necessary to a grasp of the work of art. One of the consequences of the process is the articulation of certain denotative elements.[8] Aesthetic inference is then the means by which reflective judgment proceeds; it is thus the source, logically, for the denotative structure in all such judgments.

I am not claiming that this inferential process is the only or the most distinctive facet of aesthetic experience or even that it alone establishes the denotative elements which figure in aesthetic experience. I suggest rather that it is a necessary one of those facets; and that this holds even if the reader of literature at any given point may deviate from the process, or even if its importance varies, as it seems to, for different works of literature and with different genres of art.

Evidence for this thesis is based here on a reading of an Emily Dickinson poem. It is thus centered on a single work and on a single reading; but the formal detail of the reading rather than the particular poem or interpretation is what is at issue. The poem is as follows:

> I found the phrase to every thought
> I ever had, but one;
> And that defies me, —as a hand
> Did try to chalk the sun
>
> To races nurtured in the dark;
> How would your own begin?
> Can blaze be done in cochineal,
> Or noon in mazzarin?

Our question again asks what, if anything, the poem denotes. A natural starting place for an answer to this question is by allowing to the poem's terms the denotative force they would have in the least ambitious reading possible, specifically as a description of the simple past. In "I found the phrase to every thought / I ever had but one," one would then understand an autobiographical account in which the "I" denotes a particular person who is relating a personal history. But the lines are not responsive to this interpretation, and the difficulty is hardly due to their setting in meter and rhyme. Historical writing, as Aristotle suggests in the *Poetics,* could be garnished with poetic technique and still not lose its character as history. For one thing, if the lines are supposed to serve an historical function, they serve it badly: they are notably sparse in the detail one expects from a description of matters of fact. There may be reasons why the author has omitted the detail to which an autobiographical writer would ordinarily be attentive. But even if such reasons were assumed, one might still wonder what kind of history the author *is* writing, or why she says as much as she does. The lines are meaningful if we regard them as descriptive, denoting a sequence of events in the writer's life; but they suggest of themselves the question of whether this is the way they ought to be understood.

That question is not conclusive; but the second stanza of the poem adds weight to it. "How would your own begin?" the poet asks, her question posing two directives for the reader. First, the question presupposes the lines before it. "Your own what?" the reader asks and is referred back to the opening stanza and the difficulty of the "I" in "chalking the sun." A connection is thus implied between the sections of the poem, suggesting that a cumulative process incorporating the first stanza in a grasp of the second must figure in the reading. The second directive follows from the appeal made to an unspecified "you" for testimony to the "I's" difficulty. Again, the "you" may denote a particular person; there may be reasons again why the author fails to identify him. But the possibility also exists that the "you" is anonymous by design and because its denotation is an abstract or even collective "you." The "you," then, may or may not be bound to a particular historical framework. If we take the poet to be speaking in an actual present (and thus about an historical past), the "you" would undoubtedly be placed in that present as well; but if the condition does not hold, the consequence will also alter.

The interpretation of the "you" as specific would hold so long as we continued to read the poem as history. But the objection against such a reading of the poem's opening lines applies also for the later ones, that is, the difficulty in accounting for details included and excluded. Why, after all, a question, if we are reading a description? and why, again, the sparseness of the historical context? The alternative cited gains support from the last lines of the poem: "Can blaze be done in cochineal, / Or noon in mazzarin?"—questions which, it seems from their rhetorical force, are neither directed to a particular "you" nor are reflective of mere personal expression. They ask, in general, whether those colors are able to "paint" the events mentioned (implying, of course, that they cannot). It becomes the more probable, then, that something else is at stake in the poem than the autobiography of the "I" who appears in the opening lines. Perhaps we could interpret the last lines as "*I* cannot do blaze in cochineal," etc.; but this strains the lines markedly, certainly as we *limit* the meaning to this. Thus, the last lines also suggest a generalization of denotation, an insistence that they be taken apart from the specific context of the poet's person or experience.

To read the poem through a process that moves from a beginning to an end, in the course of which we put together these interpretive cues, is in effect to identify a dialectic which no more than originates with the "I" as denoting the writer. The process soon involves a second term, the "you," reinforcing the suspicion that the reference of the "I" is not an historical reference at all. The poem concludes with an appeal that we understand to be directed to no particular person, an assurance which reflects backward to the poem's earlier lines. The emergent relation between the "I" and the "you" seems to intimate a development accomplished in the poem as a whole, from understanding which could reasonably originate with a regard for events in a specific historical context to an understanding in which what is denoted is a variable and generalized range of experience. In that shift, the historical "I" gives way to a nonspecific referent, which although set in a context, is not bound temporally or spatially as an historical individual or event would be; the referent marks the outline of a form of experience, a possible set of objects and relations to the actual definition of which it invites the reader. Thus, for example, can be understood the point of the conclusion to which a critic, Donald Thackrey, comes in his representation of the poem as suggesting that "the truly significant things in human experience dwell . . . in the realm of silence and secrecy." [9] This instance of reflective judgment, inferring a certain general range of denotation from the poem, may or may not be adequate to it; but it is the formal quality of its assertion which is at issue. On this point Thackrey's conclusion is relevant; and his conclusion is possible, it seems, only as an outcome of the kind of procedure described. What the terms of his conclusion denote are not events simply located in historical space and time, although at some far remove the occurrence of such individual events may be a condition for both the existence and the recognition of what is denoted; in this stage of reflective judgment, the events or objects exhibit themselves as general possibilities. (These possibilities, it will be further asserted in chapters 4 and 5, have a characteristic intentional modality that distinguishes them from merely logical or abstract possibilities.)

It may be objected that the process indicated, in which the reader is progressively driven away from the literal denotation of "I" and "you," is peculiar to the poem quoted. But the form of that dialectic as it is required for a grasp of Emily Dickinson's poem is characteristic, I contend, of a process bound to the reading of literature. There is, for any written word, a functional choice as to how the reader shall take it. The context of the word, while it may limit these choices, cannot explicitly decide among them, since the context itself must also be part of a context; the reader would then be obliged to see how the directions given by the latter context are to be understood. The choices thus opened to the reader are, however, not indefinite. One possibility is that the function of language should be regarded as literally descriptive and no more than that, its individual terms denoting historically locatable objects or relations, and its whole, then, their conjunction. But in the example cited this alternative fails. The interdependence of the elements of the poem, the directions which they give to the reader, suggest both that something *is* denoted by the poem and that this denotation will not be discerned so long as we address only its isolated terms. The alternative to admitting the cumulative process of aesthetic inference (it is finally on this basis that the argument here rests) is that the poem's denotation is restricted to the denotation of its terms aside from the poem. But so to limit understanding in the example cited places severe and arbitrary restrictions on the reading of the poem. It begs the question, of course, to argue that a consequence of such restrictions would be the turning of poetry into history; but the fact that we commonly acknowledge their difference reflects a distinctive possibility in the working of literary forms. That possibility may finally be rejected; but there must be some other justification for doing this than the simple assertion that literary terms and connectives can be rendered and understood as the terms and connectives of historical description.

The identification of the process of aesthetic inference is not an application of a metaphor. The opening lines of a work, if the poem referred to is an indication, initiate a number of possibilities of meaning for the individual terms and lines of the work and for the whole of which they are to be part. Those possibilities are revised and narrowed as the reader comes closer to the literal end of the poem. The evidence of the poem's detail yields an emergent principle of inclusion and exclusion, the same principle which presents itself, completed, as the reflective judgment on the poem that finally gives it life for the reader. The "I" of the opening line in the poem quoted may be Emily Dickinson, or it may denote someone else; by the end of the poem we can be reasonably certain that the poem does not have Emily Dickinson or her personal beliefs for its object. Rather we recognize themes which place those components in a general design which may designate personal elements of the reader as well: it is their generality which appears as a quantifier, the fact that they are not merely descriptive or historical. Aristotle, when he writes that poetry is more universal than history, is not legislating a distinction. He is describing the way in which poetry is taken, how the reader finds it; in a sense, he is reflecting on the fact *that* the reader finds it.

One might go so far as to argue that the poem quoted catches at the reader precisely because it is not about Emily Dickinson. (From the standpoint of a biographer, whether or not it is about her is surely a significant issue, but biography is no more an aesthetic issue than the quality of paper on which the poem is printed.) In intention—and I mean here the work's intention, not the author's—and in function, the poem moves beyond the writer's own context, engaging the reader by its dissociation from simply historical description. One important rule-of-thumb among tests of aesthetic value, that of endurance, turns largely on this generalized character of literature, as the individual work is measured by what is held significant to readers of diverse backgrounds and times. (Thus also the distinction between such works and others which are "historically" important for their influence on the evaluation of artistic forms.) An original and literal "I" may be, in Dewey's terms,[10] the "subject" of certain lines or of a poem as a whole; but even if it were the subject, this would not make it the "substance" of the poem, or what I have referred to as its aesthetic or latent denotation.

Words in isolation may be granted a range of denotative force; and statements composed of such terms will then incorporate the denotation of the units which comprise them. This does not mean that the statements themselves denote, but it does mean that they, and in turn whatever they imply involve a denotative function. The literary work of art deploys a sequence of statements in which the denotation of terms in isolation is progressively modified by connections among them; in the larger units to which aesthetic inference draws the reader, those first elements of denotation remain only a starting point. The expectations of the reader, set first as he reads the opening lines of the poem, are progressively revised and fleshed out until a conclusion of judgment is reached which encompasses the elements and process that led up to it. In the absence of such a process, we would be left with a number of independent elements arbitrarily organized, so it must seem, into a group, no single one of which depends on any other one and no member of which, except by accident, reveals a common or related intention to any other. But this, quite simply, is not literature as we know it.

This thesis is demonstrated sharply in the standard example of the spectator who, watching a melodrama, rushes onto the stage to defend the threatened heroine from the attack of the villain. Kazantzakis describes how, in a theater he visited in his childhood, a sign had been posted warning against this: "No matter what you see, do not be disturbed. It's all imaginary." Whatever we take "imaginary" to mean, the spectator's mistake is clear: he has understood one aspect of the denotation of the words spoken, but he has not understood that this is indeed an aspect. Recognition of a dislocation from simple historical process is a necessary point of departure for aesthetic inference; this is no less the case if its justification has to be found in the process of that inference itself. A condition for grasping the work in its aesthetic character is the recognition that the villain's attack is not going on in physical fact and that the presentation is thus not relevant to the physical fate of the heroine, who may or may not be virtuous and defenseless. The substance of the play is

110

sufficiently broad, one can say in retrospect, to involve the spectator without committing him to the defense of the heroine.

The reading of the Dickinson poem offers only a formal basis for the thesis that all literary works of art yield to some such analysis. But the formal basis makes a general claim. Aesthetic inference is pertinent to the reading of that poem not because of idiosyncracies in the poem but because there seems to be no alternative means of approaching it *as* a poem. Its elements are comprehensible individually; but taken together, seen in their effect on each other, they yield another level of understanding, which goes beyond the elements themselves. There is and can be no necessity that binds a reader to this process; there is only a possibility and the recommendation which a meeting with the literary work itself gives. In this sense the discovery of the force of literature is an accident; what many artists have said about their individual creations—that "they do not seek, they find" (Picasso's phrase)—seems also true of the response that art commands in general. Like any genetic account, however, this fact about the origin of art does not establish the character or value of its function. To start with the question of what the poem "amounts to," which is a reason for starting to read anything, is also to suppose a connection among its parts. The process of inference and its suggestion that the substance of the work will be something other than its subjects fairly impose themselves on the reader. The poem which starts with a problematic "I" does not, we have seen, conclude with it; the drama which introduces its subject as Hamlet the prince ends by giving life to a pattern of experience quite separable from that Hamlet who may histori-cally have never existed.[11]

Perhaps we need not invoke this process; but one can only inquire, in its appeal to practice, about an alternative to it. A poem *may* be read, even in a language unknown to the reader, for its metrics or rhyme; but although to grasp them is surely to encounter the poem at one of its levels, there is little sense in arguing that there is no more than this to its power. As we find in any individual sentence the accumulated force and articulation of its elements, so we find in the literary work as a whole a cumulative force impelled by progressively larger demands of coherence. The denotation of the work may be multiple and complex. There will be works of art, furthermore, which are so subtle or obscure that it is difficult to establish the terms of their denotation; there are others, perhaps even all of them, as certain "New Critics" have argued, where ambiguity of denotation is an intrinsic feature of their import. But to discover the coherence among its elements and what that coherence denotes, even if it includes such ambiguity, is a feature of the reading. The unity in the viewer's grasp of the work, whatever else it portends, is a function of the process of inference; what the work denotes is articulated in the assertions of that process. Inference thus reveals the terms, as well as the fact, of aesthetic denotation.

The question naturally arises at this point as to precisely what it is that the work of art denotes; and the difficulties in answering that question are in part generated by its own single-mindedness: the question itself seems to be looking for a single thing or set of properties. But if the concept of aesthetic inference as defined so far for the literary work serves as a model, the work's denotation if it is not quite as diverse as an itemized compilation of all the individual elements of the work would leave it, still may involve a considerable variety of objects and qualities, as various potentially as are the limits of conceptualization and artistic inventiveness. The process of aesthetic inference articulates the structure and themes "implied" by the object encountered by the viewer. Those themes denote—well, whatever themes denote. It may be that certain aspects of experience offer themselves as subjects more readily to art than to other means of expression and to certain arts rather than to others. But what these forms of denotation are is a question apart from that of the modality of aesthetic inference and denotation; it is the latter issue which is fundamental to the analysis undertaken here.

Aesthetic Inference and the "Heresy of Paraphrase." A number of objections to this account of aesthetic inference can be anticipated; they also provide an occasion for elaborating on the account itself. One such objection is summarized in Cleanth

Brooks's attack on the "heresy of paraphrase," [12] an argument to the effect that any attempt to make the literary work explicit and discursive is doomed beforehand and thus misbegotten in practice. Paraphrase, Brooks acknowledges—and the term describes for him a process roughly equivalent to aesthetic inference—may be helpful in walking the periphery of the literary work. The real meaning of the poem, however, is no such ancillary or posthumous statement but the work itself: we seek, in the reading, not a formulation about the poem but the poem itself. Brooks's account thus denies the aesthetic character of the inference I have described, both in its conclusions and in its process; to impose such a method in the reading of literature is for him to subordinate the object to extra-literary or extra-artistic analysis, that of "science or philosophy or theology." The literary work of art is autonomous; if we mistake this, we mistake it.

In one respect, Brooks's objection and the account given of aesthetic inference are not incompatible. No claim has been made that the conclusions which that inference reaches are literally identical with the lines of the poem from which they are drawn or that they exhaust its possibilities for experience. To "put the right word in the right place," in the first place, is the poet's virtue; and the critic, although he may write another poem, could not even then write the one he interprets. But in a different sense, Brooks's objection is misleading. Brooks reiterates that the paraphrase of a work is distinct from its real meaning, implying that its real meaning will be accessible by some alternative means to that of aesthetic inference. But it is a pertinent question as to what we can make of a meaning which defies translation or paraphrase and which apparently does not presuppose any discursive process of articulation. This counter-argument points finally to the basic methodological question of how the meaning about which Brooks writes (the real meaning—in contrast, one supposes, to the less- or un-real meaning) comes alive in the reader's experience.

The single alternative to the process of inference described, since Brooks does not deny aesthetic meaning as such, is that significance figures in the poem as immediately clear and apprehensible, and thus as effective noninferentially. As a description of the physical process of the reading of literature, this assumption simply seems false: the reading of a work is at least that—a cumulative, temporal process. Moreover, even if we admit Brooks's objection as based on a version of what Susanne Langer calls art's "virtual" time—the time within art as distinct from the time in which art is and is read—it remains problematic. For what he would be arguing then is that a grasp of the literary work resembles the account sometimes given of how we immediately apprehend the look on someone's face; that there is no transition between the temporal process of the physical reading and the work's artistic immediacy and cotemporality; and that for aesthetic significance, the latter is all that matters. The thesis thus would turn on a central issue in the theory of perception, one which figured largely in the development of gestalt psychology and its claim that perception is not fundamentally a process at all, but atemporal, the apprehension of structured fields rather than a construction of elements.[13] Even on these terms there need be no conflict with the account given here of aesthetic inference: so long as new patterns of perception stand in some nonarbitrary and thus cumulative relation to previous ones, a version of aesthetic inference may apply. Even this attenuation, however, seems unnecessary to make the case so far as literature is concerned. What is apprehended in literature is not simply a form; it is, well before that form coalesces, a complex of words and ideas. If the latter do eventually constitute a whole, the way in which they constitute it is not irrelevant to a grasp of what that whole amounts to.

Brooks's concern in arguing the heresy of paraphrase is evident: that if we admit the process and conclusions of inference as aesthetically pertinent, we must acknowledge the connection, and perhaps the equation, between the presentation of literature and certain didactic theses which could easily have been asserted by science or philosophy. And however clear it is that literature impinges on the worlds about which the scientist or philosopher talks, the differences separating the two sides are no less evident. The claims so far made for aesthetic inference may seem to ignore these differences, and it is true that no basis has been provided for marking that inference as aesthetic, except as it applies (circularly) to works of art. It is, so far, inference *simpliciter* and thus isomorphic to inference in a large class of discursive and nonaesthetic systems. It is a reasonable question, then, as to why a distinctive, "aesthetic" character should be attributed to some of these inferences, but not to others.

This issue will be discussed later in some detail, but one cautionary note is worth mentioning here concerning an assumption implicit in the statement of the heresy of paraphrase. The assumption is that because certain common elements figure in all the various types of inference, no other, categorial differences can separate them. But this assumption goes beyond and finally against the evidence. One of our later theses may be anticipated as an example of what that evidence might be—that the reader of literature, as opposed to the reader of a psychological analysis, for example, does not primarily, if at all, follow the general conclusions of aesthetic inference to a theoretical end. The features of the judgment that engage him, as distinct from their counterparts in theoretical analysis, substitute for the latter's disclosure of generality and atemporality a claim of immediacy and process. Grammatically or syntactically equivalent judgments, to put the argument more generally, may serve various functions. The end of scientific discourse is commonly taken to be understanding; the end of art and its appearance in aesthetic experience, I shall argue, is closer to a practical activity, a doing. The heresy of paraphrase suggests that if discursive inference is aesthetically relevant, then since a similar process is relevant to the work of science, it follows that the conclusions of the two processes have the same theoretical status. But that conclusion would be mistaken if other processes impinged, without denying the process, at that juncture, on the process of inference; for it might be *there* that the aesthetic source was located. This represents a possible solution to the legitimate objections raised in the accusation of the heresy of paraphrase; the actual form of that solution is elaborated in chapter 4.

Denotation: Analogies and Dissonance Among the Arts. The suggestion has been made that although this essay draws primarily on the evidence of literary works of art, its conclusions bear on the question of the denotative status of the other arts as well. That relevance can scarcely be defined for each of the arts; nor do I attempt here to consider the special case of natural beauty. It is possible, however, by relating the foregoing analysis to certain other arts, and particularly to painting and music, to indicate its potential generality, as well as the problems which the attempt to raise it to the level of a general theory must face.

The question of their denotative status does not arise so readily with respect to the other arts as it does for literature. This difference undoubtedly reflects differences in the media themselves, specifically the absence from those other arts of the discursive least elements—the words—which comprise the literary work. It has been argued here, however, that those discursive elements serve in the medium of literature as *data* for the process of inference, not in any sense as the *conclusions* of that inference or as the reflective judgment which those conclusions comprise. This phenomenon suggests a possible link between the account of literary denotation and denotation in the nonliterary arts. If the discursive elements in literature are the raw material from which the denotation of individual works emerges, it is not the individual words or even the individual clauses or sentences which isolate or identify that denotation. Inferences are drawn as the units of the work are cumulatively articulated, as the first-level properties (discursive and nondiscursive) of those units (dictionary meanings, rhyme, color) are distinguished and then brought together in progressively larger units. Thus, the possibility that aesthetic inference figures in arts like painting or music does not depend on the absence from the nonliterary arts of *linguistic* units of syntax—an obvious difference—but on the question of whether such syntactic elements as *are* present in them may yield discursive themes which can be either verbally or nonverbally articulated. Those themes or propositions might be open to verbal formulation even where the syntactic units themselves are not, if only an index of translation could be established; still in the absence of such an index, we might find it possible and useful to speak of discursive but nonverbal themes or propositions.

The grounds for holding that aesthetic inference is a feature of judgments directed to representational painting differ only slightly from the grounds cited in the instance of literature. Although the subjects are not mentioned in painting as they may be in literary discourse, that is, they are not named, they are sufficiently well identified to yield conclusions on a work's substance or denotation formally similar to those drawn with respect to literature. The syntactic elements in Masaccio's fresco of the expulsion of Adam and Eve from Eden are not less explicit, although they are less complex, than those in Milton's representation of Adam and Eve in *Paradise Lost*. One would not take seriously a judgment of the fresco which referred to its subject as Cain and Abel—and this would be based on the internal evidence (for example, that one of the figures in it is female). Nor would one credit the judgment that the fresco represents the incident of the expulsion as comic. A procedure similar to the one invoked in the reading of Emily Dickinson's poem seems, in fact, to operate in the viewing described. It is difficult to imagine how otherwise a viewer's judgment concerning the tragic expulsion, of its effect on Adam and Eve as Masaccio has portrayed them, could be derived; and it is plain that such judgment is integral to the view. Perhaps we *need* not refer to it even if it is *possible* to do so: it has been suggested for the literary work as well that a reader can confine his attention to syntactic elements like meter or rhythm to the exclusion of others. In a representational painting, one may, then, look only to color and linear balance. But, as in the earlier case, there is reason for supposing that this will not provide an adequate grasp of the work. It may be said, without straining the metaphor, that, as Gombrich notes, we *read* the painting[14] and not only in flat, nonverbal terms. The individual painting, at whatever point we break into it, offers a number of alternative interpretations with regard to its subject. The judgment of the painting progressively narrows these alternatives until the terms of its denotation and in effect the painting itself as object emerges. "Reading a picture," Gombrich writes in the essay just cited, "is a piecemeal affair that starts with random shots, and these are followed by the search for a coherent whole." This process approximates the stages of inference described above for the Dickinson poem, as well as the linkage cited earlier between syntactic and reflective elements in Wittkower's account of the Bernini sculptures.

This methodological analogy does not imply that the conclusions of aesthetic inference for painting are typically identical to those drawn from the literary work; they seem to be characteristically more modest. It would be difficult, for example, to conceive of a painting which implied the conclusions attributed by Thackrey to even so simple a poem as the one quoted. This disparity must be the more imposing, the larger the scope of the literary work, as, for instance, in the cases of *War and Peace* or *Ulysses*. One reason for this is that literary works are typically more complex than works of painting in terms of the sheer number of syntactical units, their consistencies and implications, that figure in literary composition. The reflective judgments articulated may then be expected to be proportionately more complex, and also more explicit in isolating the terms of the work's denotation.

This difference, based on numbers, is not the only factor in the variant emphases of aesthetic inference for the reading of painting and the reading of literature, however. The quality of the syntactic elements remains a more fundamental factor. The words of literature, even if they serve primarily as data for any eventual judgment, nonetheless shape that judgment and its objects: the relationship, we have seen, is inferential. Also included in the complexity of the elements of the literary work are, for example, modal connectives. Not only objects and qualities are denoted; assertive relations, that such-and-such is or is not the case, appear in reflective judgments on literature.

It seems evident that if such operators are found at all among the data, and thus, eventually in the denotation, of painting, they are less common. The syntactic elements of painting emphasize a rather different aspect: not the modalities of relation but the qualities or objects themselves and the abstractions directly bound to them. This comes clear as, in the examples cited, we find ourselves speaking of the look or seeming of the work of visual art. Such a look, as of anguish or contrition, may characterize either individual parts of the work or the work as a whole; they thus provide an element which although not absent from literature is overshadowed by the articulation of its connectives. The literary work emphasizes *re*presentation rather than presentation; the sheer appearance of certain qualities is more characteristic a feature of painting than it is of writing, although it is not absent from the latter. The sources of reflective judgment in painting come closer than those of literature to being "iconic" signs[15] which denote by pointing to themselves rather than to other referents. The latter feature is not absent from literature, but is of lesser importance there. It is as though the "handles" with which painting provides its audience are less numerous, less conveniently located, less versatile; the ends to which its audience can "take" the inferences from painting are proportionately restricted.

This restriction amounts to a limitation on the denotative force of painting, however, not to its exclusion. A work of literature implies assertions which denote groups of objects, properties, and relations—for example, in the Dickinson poem, the assertion that important moments of experience are inexplicable. Such judgments denote because of the conventions of denotation which figure in language in the first place. The work of plastic arts, more obviously, depends on a look or semblance; but a denotative factor analogous to the one ascribed to literature is present here as well. The look of contrition, for example, is hardly the end or totality of the emotion itself; the totality involves more than only that look. Even if it is the latter to which the painting or piece of sculpture is apparently restricted, this does not fix the limits either of the object or of the audience's grasp. To note contrition in the work is to have inferred its presence from the available cues; the process of inference acts not only to bring together those cues, but also to deepen and to generalize their reference. It is not simply a look which Bernini's sculptures present but that which the look is of; it is not only Mary Magdalene's contrition which is designated there but contrition. Such qualities, general in the same way that what is denoted in literature tends beyond any specifically historical occurrence, comprise the primary form of denotation for the visual arts. The process of generalization is close to that previously described, even if the syntactic terms supporting the inference are nonverbal or less verbal. The anguish of a painted figure as projected by reflective judgment does not call on the viewer for a direct practical response to an historical event—for example, for a word of sympathy—precisely because it is no real person, historically located, who is in anguish but a painted one. This distinction may be less clear in some types of painting, such as portrait painting, than in poetry. But even viewers of a portrait are less concerned with the portrait as a likeness than with the qualities evident in the painting as painting—the more so, the better the painting. What is painted implies that "this is what anguish is"; the implication, if nothing else, distinguishes emotion seen in the painting from anyone's personal emotion or from a particular historical instance of emotion.

The objections may be raised to this account of the denotation of painting first, that there is no reason for restricting it to painting, that any expression, including, for example, that on a "real" face, will denote in the same way that representation in the plastic arts have been said to; or, secondly, that the account given posits a "ghost in the machine," the real emotion which its appearance only denotes. But, with respect to the first of these, both the look of a painting and the look of a person may and almost invariably do refer the viewer to something more than only that look. I have not been arguing that painting is unique in this property, only that it has it. What painting distinctively provides is the generalized force proposed here as a characteristic feature of aesthetic denotation; this feature articulates the qualities of the painting as general, in contrast to the look of the individual which designates primarily his emotion. As strongly as a viewer may react to the denotation of the painting, it is not or at least is not only a personal quality or emotion to which he responds. Furthermore, this does not imply the presence of a ghost in the machine, a real emotion or state of consciousness which the quality remarked in the painting stands for. Again, like expression outside of art, expression within art needs to be understood not as the consequence of some otherwise invisible state, but as an aspect of that state. Thus, one need not claim, in following this account of denotation, that a painting denotes something other than itself, as, for example, feeling which is distinct from any look. But it is consistent with this to claim that the appearance of certain qualities in a work of visual art refers the viewer (i.e., denotes) to a larger range of experience of which those first qualities are only an aspect. That larger range of experience is not more real than the appearance or historically or systematically prior to it—but the appearance forces our awareness of it.

With nonrepresentational or abstract painting and with music, the problem of identifying the syntactic elements in which aesthetic inference originates is increasingly difficult, not formally, since the formal requirements demand only that the whole should be comprised of individual elements related in a serial process and the whole subsumable under a single principle, but substantively, so far as concerns the *signification* of those elements. Syntactic elements are evident in the media referred to, for instance, their rhythm and balance. But it is less clear that these elements in music and abstract painting direct attention to some thing denoted beyond their own exhibitive character. Colors and geometric patterns, rhythm and counterpoint, can be isolated and identified in the works of these arts. The articulation of aesthetic inference, however, which diminishes even in the distance between literature and representational painting, seems in these other forms to be more restricted still. It becomes a serious question as to whether their syntactic components serve a comparable function at all to those of the works of literature or of representational painting.

In some music this question may seem to yield more readily than it in fact does. The syntactic elements of program music or of music set to words may be taken to cohere in a manner analogous to the elements of the literary arts. Thus, we know the fountains of Rome which provided the motif for Respighi's work and the paintings by Hartmann which inspired Moussorgsky in his "Pictures at an Exhibition." Knowing them, it is then possible to argue that the parts of the musical piece denote the sources. But even for such examples, and a fortiori in less programmatic works, the question persists as to whether their appreciation is significantly affected by an awareness of such references. Perhaps it is; but even if we allow that claim in some cases, it has less force than comparable claims would for virtually any work of literature or representational painting. This diminished relevance reflects the problematic status of reflective judgment as it supervenes on music's syntactic elements. It may be possible, after the fact, to see how the themes in "The Fountains of Rome" denote those fountains. But there is little evidence that even a sensitive listener, before he knew this, would reach that conclusion; and his failure cannot be passed off as due to the listener's ignorance of a vocabulary, since it is the existence of such a vocabulary which is in question. Instances abound, furthermore, where knowledge of the historical circumstance of composition or statements of the artist's intentions for his work may be misleading: so, for example, the questionable denotative conception, even though it comes from Beethoven himself, of his opening theme in the Fifth Symphony as "Fate knocking at the door."

It is often suggested that we may find or hear that a certain piece of music is sad, for example, or represents or expresses sadness. But such characterization is usually imprecise and often contested; it does not, in any event, figure in most responses to a large number of important musical works, to much of Bach, for example. Where in representational painting the figures may be unmistakable and the qualities of their expression only slightly less so—a contrast in itself to literature where more complex theses are exhibited—we seem further restricted in music and in other art forms which resemble it in this respect, for example, in abstract paintings and in objects of the decorative arts like Persian rugs and jewelry.[16]

It might be claimed that music and similarly abstract art forms, by their internal articulation of space and time, denote objects or perhaps only shapes for the definition of which those rather spare categories by themselves suffice. This on the surface may seem an empty assertion even if true, since the question would still follow of how such denotation was pertinent to aesthetic judgment. But the question at issue here is not whether the arts together or individually denote an unusual or interesting set of objects or qualities, but whether—given the hints supplied by inference as we locate its process in the literary work—they can be said to denote *at all.* It is obviously not a proof that this is the case to claim that any art object effects a pattern of coherence among certain minimal categories such as space or time which then may denote for an audience some one of the things in their range of experience whose character was determined by those fundamental categories. But there is some fragmentary evidence that this is the case. The many attempts from Plato to Susanne Langer to establish the denotative import of music may be incomplete; yet the attempts themselves are not arbitrary. If they are juxtaposed to the hints provided by the analysis of denotation in other of the arts; if they are viewed in light of the explanation given in the following chapters of how that denotation realizes its aesthetic character; and if, furthermore, one takes seriously the evidence of common determinant patterns relating objects stylistically and thematically, although the objects come from quite different arts,[17] then we may—arguing backwards—yet make sense of a denotational scheme for those arts to which it is less obviously pertinent as well as for those in which the presence and importance of denotation is unquestionable.

The latter comments are admittedly no more than suggestive. They tell something, furthermore, of the price which a theory pays as it looks for completeness in the data which stand at its periphery. A fundamental issue which this account of inference and denotation must yet face, however broadly the account applies, is how it explains, after all the conclusions of any particular reflective judgment are drawn, the peculiar power exerted by those judgments and, finally, by the aesthetic object. A type of inference has been named, but it has not been shown to be aesthetic in any distinctive sense; the generalized form of denotation ascribed to art, although distinguished from historical denotation, yet seems very much like other generalized or universal forms. As the account stands, then, the question behind Brooks's account of the heresy of paraphrase persists. To say that the work of art denotes, and to say that this denotation becomes evident as the consequence of a process of inference, does nothing to distinguish the features of aesthetic denotation or aesthetic inference from the ordinary garden varieties. It may yet turn out that there *is* no difference, that what separates the work of art from other objects is not related to its cognitive status at all. This question, then, remains to be faced. In its largest reach it asks how it is possible that a work of art denotes: what about it, as distinct from other "things" (geraniums, people, sociological theories) gives it this power? That question is the more pressing in light of the difficulties encountered in the analysis of denotation in the various arts. Until we consider it, the contention that literature, for instance, differs only quantitatively with respect to the explicitness of its denoting from the more abstract arts is of limited force. In the absence of such analysis denotation can be viewed as accidental to any object of which it is a feature and thus not as intrinsic to the role of the object as a source of aesthetic value. Only after considering this question, furthermore, will we be able to test the claim that what we find in this account of aesthetic inference provides a clue to the general character of aesthetic experience. Perhaps art is not one thing, but essentially many things; perhaps even those many things are many other things; and perhaps, finally, even if we were to succeed in identifying common features of what we ordinarily call art, we should be but temporizing with more central issues still, concerning, for example, the derivation of concepts or categories. But these possibilities, if they represent dangers to the inquiry, also underscore the importance of seeing where it leads.

The Arrow's Pointing. Certain formal conclusions can be drawn from the discussion thus far. The account given of aesthetic inference proceeds readily enough where the units contributing to the process are transparent, in the cases of words or figures. Difficulties mount in fixing the denotation of a work of art as words or figures are wanting, and it may be assumed that these difficulties occur because of the absence of such units. But a likelier explanation, it now turns out, is not that something present in certain of the arts is lacking in others, but that the role which that something—the syntactic elements—played in literature, for example, had not been clear; the linguistic element may mistakenly have been thought to contribute *everything* to the emergence of art's denotation, when only one feature of the linguistic element was involved—and that, one which is possessed by other, nonlinguistic syntactic elements as well. In other words, just as the denotative object in literature may not be itself named among the syntactic elements from which it emerges, so in the other arts denotation does not turn on a naming function which, as nonlinguistic, those other arts cannot provide. This does not establish that they are denotative; it only rules out one common ground for *asserting* that they are not.

A specific reason appears for caution in addressing the question of the cognitive status of art. That reason takes shape in the process of aesthetic inference and more concisely in the epigraphs cited at the beginning of this chapter from Plato and Wittgenstein. We find in those sources the suggestion that denotation turns only indirectly on the literal denotation of the elements of what does the denoting;[18] that it is rather as a *function* of those elements that the comprehension of the audience takes hold. The fact that certain media of art do not make use of words does not preclude their having denotative force or imply an essential difference between the media of which they are part and other media. The possibility remains of a symmetry or isomorphism along quite different lines; whether such symmetry exists or not can only be decided as we see what makes denotation possible and effective in those cases for which there is no question that it is present, and as we may then undertake the difficult critical task of applying such conclusions to works or media of art for which they are less obviously pertinent.

The silence of what we find before us, in the written word and painted figure and even in the musical sound, proves to be a starting point for the fact and the analysis of aesthetic inference —that, rather than the superficially transparent and articulate symbols or signs which only certain of the media deploy. This does not mean that literal denotation is without significance for the phenomenon of aesthetic denotation. It means, however, that to limit the analysis of the latter to its literal elements is to beg a prior question, namely, whether it is in these elements, given and taken literally, that we locate the basis for art's cognitive status. An affirmative answer to this prior question, it seems now, contradicts the prima facie evidence and some of the systematic evidence behind that; it is from a tactical vantage point which takes such evidence seriously that Plato and Wittgenstein speak. Art, we may find, communicates to a variety of ends and through diverse vehicles. But it does not in any of them speak about what it is saying. If it is to refer to something, if it is to denote, the viewer himself serves as an agent not only in understanding the process but in the process itself. The claims of the work, in other words, do not simply present themselves as its physical components perhaps do. To realize what the former are means to grasp the articulation of those components, a grasp which is itself a form of articulation.

It is probably true that whatever its relevance, aesthetic inference alone does not account for all of the facets of aesthetic experience; other less linear or discursive elements are undoubtedly significant among the elements of the art work, and perhaps they contribute as well to its cognitive status. We may suspect, furthermore, that substantial differences occur among the arts and even within individual art forms with respect to the role of aesthetic inference. But these qualifications are less a criticism of the concept than an indication of the need to know what in the aesthetic object makes aesthetic inference possible. Through such analysis we may expect to learn something as well about the actual content and conclusions of aesthetic inference. So far, a question has been raised about its form; the substantive issue is open. Such qualifications notwithstanding, one negative justification which has figured in this discussion will carry over to any elaboration of the thesis that aesthetic inference and the denotative force of the judgments in which it concludes are integral elements of the encounter with art: the prospect of that encounter without them.

The Work in Process

One generalization stands out, in all the attempts to explain man's interest in creating and enjoying art, and that is that the interest exists. The accounts of this interest are moot: man may or may not by nature be an imitator; perhaps there is nothing edifying in the description of him as homo faber or ludens; Eros, we can argue with the Freudian or, before him, with the Platonist, is an inspiration only symptomatic of some other, more fundamental impulse. The fact itself remains: that much energy and time are spent on the artistic commodity. Critics will dispute whether the earth in Earthworks or the silence on which John Cage plays are the stuff from which art emerges; or if, on the other side, it is not the creations of modern advertising which address the pleasures of its audience as the cave paintings of Lascaux did for their audience. Museums and libraries, the curricula of universities, and books of criticism (some about criticism), offer testimony of art's past if not its presence; but in the long run from the present they are probably the least of it. We may be mistaken even as to what the living art forms are (this self-concealment as a feature of the real art); but if we were mistaken about their very existence, past or present, there would be little else that we might count on.

And no less persistent is the need to understand them. Here what stands first in silence, as mere appearance, soon begins to testify, to articulate the possibilities. We see that art, some art, means, comes to a point, denotes; we see this as readily, perhaps in the same movement, as we feel what art does. Yet meaning has many vehicles, and most of them are not art. If we go only by the

128

weight of numbers, we may stop with a dictionary of denotative terms, and art itself, except as a word, probably will not appear here: witness for contrast the objects of art in the reference room of any library. Art, it seems, deploys its significance differently. We need always, for example, to look at it and not at a surrogate; its demands place themselves not piecemeal but whole; it initiates action but action performed as an audience sits still. An exotic appearance, however one wishes to save it.

There is, to be sure, opposition to saving it at all, at least to saving this particular appearance. Such opposition seizes on the fragmentary reports taken from literature and uses them against art. So we may hear Objection A: what asserts itself in literature simply does not in other places—in paper flowers and in wallpaper, in Persian rugs and in earrings. Art all (no doubt), but as removed from meaning or denotation as nonmeaning or denotation can be. Thus, a rather different appearance. An answer to such objection need be evasive only in the part which postpones talking about all of art; the other part recalls that even with literature as principal, the elements of significance show themselves as neither simple nor self-evident. We have, it seems, to learn to find them. And so the search, already begun, extends to see how meanings can possibly serve art's purpose. The whole will be a step further toward the meaning of meaning itself—and not only for literature.

Objection B: that the significance of literature as model, far from giving the clue to the working of art, supports only its own exclusion. Literature, so the good formalist patronizes it, may be worthy and alive but is either the least of the arts or even well outside them. The difficulty in appraising this objection is that a priori arguments can be contested only by others. There is no way, we see in this, of disproving the assessment or even of disputing it, except perhaps by exhibiting the qualities in terms of which distinctions are ever made. Is it so strange to speak of types of experience (as well as of types)?

The question, then, is larger than those roused simply in the appreciation of art. The one possibility of surmounting it is if we can know the elements—and below that, any one element—of which the distinctiveness in the difference is made, and for what end. It may be, understanding hopes, that some differences among the varieties of significance are more different than others. Perhaps even Ur-Differences. That, at least, can be measured. So long as we do not expect to find them as legislative, or as substance, we may yet find them as practiced.

A judgment on an object of taste can be quite disinterested and yet very interesting.

Kant, *Critique of Judgment*

An existing individual . . . thinks everything in relation to himself, being infinitely interested in existing.

Kierkegaard, *Concluding Unscientific Postscripts*

The innocent eye is a myth.

E. H. Gombrich, *Art and Illusion*

4

Aesthetic Proximity: The Occasion of Belief

A prominent element in analyses of aesthetic experience since the end of the eighteenth century has been the attempt to reconstruct that experience in terms of the categories of disinterest or detachment or distance.[1] It is not, on these accounts, the intensity of the experience or the prospect of an "aesthetic education" which is viewed as characteristic, but rather an attitude of disinterest which, as it purportedly defines a characteristic distance between the audience of art and its objects (also purportedly) defines the boundary between aesthetic and nonaesthetic varieties of experience. On some such accounts, recognition of the phenomenon of disinterest is a necessary condition for the concept of art or more generally for the work of the philosophy of art; even where the phenomenon is given less weight, its pertinence is still often assumed as a matter of course. It is thus construed as a concept both clear and indisputable, or at least sufficiently so that one task of aesthetics is taken to be its elaboration.

This item of common agreement is not likely to be without foundation;[2] and I shall not be arguing against its relevance in some sense, so much as I shall be disputing the generality of the claims made for it. Clearly enough, certain features of art and of the experience it evokes support the characterization of aesthetic disinterest; but that characterization has little to say about other and, if anything, more basic facts revealed in the attractive or adhesive power of art. This power manifests itself as a phenomenon of engagement, in the *connection* of the viewer to the object rather than in the gap that separates them; there is need, if we wish to understand art whole, for looking as well or even better on the side of aesthetic proximity as on that of aesthetic distance.

The purpose of this essay, then, is to define the terms of this need. The means for defining them is located here in the role of belief as a function of the truth of art in aesthetic experience. The method is circuitous; but the hope is that by taking this avenue we may find the answer to a question that is also circuitous: *why* do the elements of reflective judgment—and finally, of art—have the force that they do? Closing in on that question, we attempt to see more clearly, as we have already attempted to see them distinctly, what those elements are.

The Brevity of Aesthetic Distance. The occasion and detail of accounts of aesthetic distance are straightforward. From looking directly at the varieties of art and from examining responses to them, our own as well as others', we see that the transactions impose certain conditions on the viewer. His attentions bear on artifacts displayed in frames: museums, concert halls, theaters; and in frames within frames: picture frames, movements of a symphony, acts of a play. The common effect of these devices is to disengage him from activities and intentions with which he is ordinarily occupied; and certainly the immediate relation between him and the objects he attends to in this way is peculiar: his feelings and his actions as the relation unfolds are at odds with what they would be in more usual circumstances. The museum-goer hardly thinks to judge the fruit in the Cézanne *Still Life* by its taste; tempted as he may be, the play-goer restrains himself from exposing Iago to Othello and thus, as he might then think, bringing about a different conclusion from the one for which the drama seems destined. The viewer, at least in some ways, is detached, insulated from aspects which the object before him could conceivably and reasonably be otherwise taken to display. It is evident, that without that insulation he would be, and would act as if he were, back in real life.

The principal systematic presupposition of most conceptions of aesthetic distance or disinterest as they attempt to account for these conditions of the projects of art is a claim for the independence of certain moments or modes of experience. That presupposition is not necessary: aesthetic distance might be measured by gradations which never reach a point of qualitative difference from other relations between perceiver and object. As a rule, however, it is the assertion of a difference in kind that has figured in accounts of aesthetic distance. Human activities, the claim goes, are explicable by a relatively small number of explanatory categories, the variations among which are substantive as well as functional; that is to say, the categorial differences reflect real differences in human faculties or senses as well as varieties in human activity.

A consequence of such analysis has been the definition of the aesthetic transaction as a "free gift," not responding to either desire or will and not yielding a cognitive or practical or moral effect. A novel or painting thus establishes itself on its own terms or, generically, on the distinctive terms of art but at any rate on no other. To judge it on moral grounds or to assess its cognitive claims is to misconstrue the quality of its presentation. Even to speak of the pleasure it gives is to open the way to confusion: aesthetic pleasure, it should be understood, is not simply the immediate pleasure of sensory gratification. Rather the activity of aesthetic judgment is *sui generis* in both process and conclusion; the measure and intensity of this character, reflected in the peculiar detachment or disinterest of an audience vis-à-vis the object, is manifest in the activities and their sources from which it dissociates itself.

Kant's, although not the first, remains the most powerful statement of this view of aesthetic judgment, as regards both its systematic detail and its consequent influence. Certain elements in the historical background of his position are relevant to an appreciation of the form of the concept. The precise extent of the influence of early eighteenth-century British thinkers like Shaftesbury and Hutcheson on Kant may remain a question, but there is no doubt of the fact itself or that the conception of aesthetic judgment already described is one which Kant drew from them. Statements such as Hutcheson's—that "the pleasure [of beauty] does not arise from any knowledge of principles, proportions, causes or of the usefulness of the object; it strikes us at first with the idea of beauty . . ." [3]—typify Kant's sources; both the internal evidence of the *Critique of Judgment* and its explicit references to the writers mentioned establish the connection.[4]

Kant's appropriation of the concept of disinterest is not accounted for only by the fact that it was available; he was inclined to welcome the concept. For one, in order for the protest against his "dogmatic" predecessors to succeed, Kant required a lever by which to break the hold of their monistic thesis concerning the nature of judgment. He adduced in this connection a variety of systematic objections based on the thesis that the tradition of Leibniz, Wolff, and Baumgarten, was, after all, dogmatic; that the foundations, such as the Principle of Sufficient Reason, on which they had built had been laid a priori; and thus that, committed beforehand to such stipulations, they could not be expected to, and did not in fact, adequately take into account the structure of experience. They may have saved themselves and even their principles but not the phenomenon and, in all events, not the phenomenon of art.

The basis of this reaction is Kant's summary of the empirical evidence; his rejection of dogmatic metaphysics is directed not only against its method but also against its conclusions: the exhibition or deduction of experience embodied in those conclusions does not reconstruct experience in fact. This empirical ground is a constant feature of Kant's conclusions on the judgment of taste, a type of judgment which Leibniz and Baumgarten take to be a low-level, "confused" cognitive judgment but which Kant asserts to be quite distinct from cognitive judgment and not confused at all. The issue for Kant is not whether the categories for rendering cognition can be tortured sufficiently to cover the judgment of taste. He contends only that the texture of aesthetic judgment differs as experience from the qualities of other species of judgment. To regard them all as one, then, is to proceed not in the absence of empirical evidence but in the face of contrary evidence. The testimony invoked by Kant—Kant is in this respect very much an ordinary language philosopher (at least of ordinary German)[5]—may be disputed, but its tenor is explicit and constant both in general (in all of the Critiques) and in particular with respect to aesthetic judgment in its linguistic and perceptual elements. A concept which provided a means of defining the differences among the types of judgment would thus have been welcome, and it is in this context that we best understand his receptivity to the claims for disinterest.

As is often the case in the migration of ideas, however, the concept of disinterest as formulated by Kant includes his own innovations. It is especially significant for understanding his position and the later appearances of aesthetic distance to note what Kant omitted in his elaboration. In Shaftesbury, the single most important figure in its development, the concept of disinterest first emerged in the discussion of ethics, selflessness being invoked as a condition of moral action.[6] The argument there, a reaction against the theological frameworks preceding it, focuses on the thesis that action performed for personal interest or gain is morally problematic. The expansion of disinterest to qualify the objective appreciation of beauty is undertaken only later by Shaftesbury—the expansion continuing as he extends the attribute of disinterest to cognitive judgment as well. The triad of the good, the beautiful, and the true thus converge to a common point under this single condition of judgment.

Shaftesbury's extension of the range of disinterest is closer in its conclusion to the dogmatic tradition than to Kant's criticism of that tradition; certainly the concept of disinterest provides no means in Shaftesbury's work for distinguishing among types or species of judgment. Kant's use of the concept to define the distinction between aesthetic and other types of judgment is thus a sharp revision of the concept's initial form. Disinterest as it evolved for Shaftesbury was an immediate quality of judgment, noncategorial and insular; this much was included in the concept when Kant restricted its applicability to aesthetic judgment which on other, independent grounds he took to be noncategorial and immediate. But Kant both reinforces the impulse governing Shaftesbury's account and restricts it to a more limited principle. Although he maintains the irrelevance of practical consequence to moral judgment, genuine disinterest, in which the object of attention is displaced from any mediate context, including that of will or desire, cannot, for Kant, be a feature of moral judgment. Nor does disinterest apply to cognitive judgment, in which, as Kant conceives of it, understanding itself is an interested purpose mediated by categories.

Partly because of Kant's influence, partly because the apparent generic distinctiveness of art led to theories parallel to his, the assertion by Kant of what is in effect an aesthetic faculty has since been almost continuously represented. In one of its reaches it figures in what Eliot called the dissociation of sensibility as that dissociation between feeling and thought reached its peak in the nineteenth century; it recurs in much of post-Kantian German aesthetics ranging from Schiller and Schopenhauer to Hanslick. It has appeared in still more radical statements by such twentieth-century writers as Fry and Bell as well as in the less explicitly related formulations of the empathy theorists (for instance, Lipps and Vernon Lee), in Santayana, I. A. Richards, and (with some straining) in Dewey and Susanne Langer. (If it seems perverse to regard emotivist positions as variations on formalism, given the emotivist criticism of formalism, in, for example, I. A. Richards and Dewey, one need only recall that in formalism as well, the judgment of taste emerges in the affective response of the spectator alone. At least there is no way of talking about the object's form without this; and there is not, furthermore, much else to be said about it.)

The drive behind such accounts in part reflects the material distinction asserted by the concept of art itself, one effect of which would have been, understandably, to reiterate and thus to underscore the distinction between aesthetic qualities and others. Thus, for example, Dewey's attribution of the discovery of the idea of art to the recognition that control and organization of the general flux of experience, the line of demarcation within its entire expanse, are possible.[7] In all such formulation what is aimed for is the uncovering of a qualitatively distinct mode of experience. The concept of disinterest, supporting the distinction, also provided a common means of rendering the contrast between art and other significant human activities.

If we wish to understand the development and currency of the concept of aesthetic distance, however, mere speculation is secondary to the systematic and prima facie evidence, some of which has already been discussed. That evidence is difficult to summarize only because of its profusion. Analyses of the source of artistic creativity, as an illustration, have as various a history as that of art itself; but even the earliest and uncritical accounts which oppose the sources of art to those of other activities verge on the concept of disinterest. The artist, we hear, is "inspired," acts through a "divine frenzy," as a tribal shaman or seer—no one of these a role generated by the will or conferred by the power of technology, and none of its results to be altered or affected by them. Again, the experience and behavior of an audience which address a work of art are distinctive: compelling as art may be, it does not move us to the obvious forms of practical action, nor is it accountable to or translatable into the theorems of conceptual analysis. The social history of the expansion of the arts relates that expansion closely to the phenomenon of leisure, to moments which escape commonplace motive and need.

One theme persists in these appearances, even in the most rudimentary statements: that the world of art is not yet or still the real world; that a difference in function, perhaps also in substance, separates its representations from reality which is matter-of-fact and consequential; that the stance and prospects of the participants in these activities differ significantly. The cave painters of Lascaux and Altamira were apparently convinced of the power over the animals portrayed which their work gave their community; and the Egyptian tomb paintings, although not intended to be viewed in this world, were meant to ease the passage of the dead. But none of these works, in fact and against all desire, themselves gave an actual object to the communities by which they were engaged—the quarry for the eating, or the dead person once again alive. And the communities which honored such instances of art could scarcely have been ignorant of that fact.

Such considerations comprise a rough background to the concept of aesthetic disinterest or distance; and assuredly we recognize in these comments the way in which some moments of art manifest themselves. Yet for all its illumination of these facets, the concept by itself both omits and fails to make provision for other facets which are no less pertinent, what is cited here as the notion of aesthetic proximity. The latter notion, abstracted from the aesthetic moment, underscores not the characteristic detachment of that moment from other modes of experience and the issues at their source, but its connections or implications; not the disinterest that marks the observer's attitude, setting him "beside" himself, but his intensity, the way in that moment of detachment that he seems to assert himself so urgently in his world. The concepts of disinterest or aesthetic distance provide a plausible basis for saying that the spectator who jumps onto the stage to protest what an actor is doing is mistaken; it gives no account of what prevents the other spectators from walking in the opposite direction, out of the theater. And surely the burden of the analysis, like the members of most audiences, will be found there. Observation alone will accord to aesthetic experience an unusual power of attraction; there is no a priori justification for holding this power to be a lesser feature of the experience than the distancing effect. If anything, the adhesive force is systematically prior to the other, since without it, the notion of disinterest would be nugatory even conceptually. To ask the concept of disinterest alone to account for the intensity or adhesion of an audience (in the language of aesthetic distance, little more could be said about it than that the audience is neither underdistanced nor overdistanced, but just at the right distance) is to require a tautology to do more work than it can.

A variety of other items of evidence underscores the need for a counterpoise to the concept of aesthetic distance. The histories of the individual arts provide substantial impetus to this need. The origins, as they can be inferred, of music or painting or literature turn on a relation between spectator, to say nothing of the artist, and object which is so close that it finally obscures the distinction between primitive religion and primitive art. Even the institutionalization of aesthetic distance through the framing devices referred to does not diminish seriously the evocation by art of an uncommon measure of concentration and intensity. Such frames undoubtedly place on the work of art restrictions, and thus on the viewer, demands, different from those asserted in the original construction: there is a difference in a listener's grasp of chamber music as the chamber in which it is played varies. But underlying these differences, a more than formal connection remains between even the newer texture of disinterest and the governing interest which is a prominent feature in the early stages of the development of the arts and a persistent feature even in the later self-consciousness exhibited in that history. The concept of aesthetic proximity serves to identify this connection. I shall argue that it is an essential complement to aesthetic distance; and that where this complementarity is not acknowledged, analyses of aesthetic experience and its objects will be at best misleading and at worst false.

One means of demonstrating this claim and of formulating the conceptual structure of aesthetic proximity is by examination of the relation between art and belief, or how the beliefs of the viewer of art characteristically affect his experience or appreciation of the work. An important aspect of the process of perceptual relations is the manner in which novel elements are integrated with elements previously grounded—how, for example, they fit prior cognitive commitments. This is a matter of special pertinence to the present discussion since the concept of aesthetic distance makes special demands on that process of integration. If aesthetic distance is to realize the autonomy required of its objects, the objects must not be implicated in other contexts than the one they themselves immediately provide. It is in accord with this condition that, virtually without exception, conceptions of aesthetic distance have been in agreement that the aesthetic transaction either does not yield even potential knowledge or that, if it does, whatever is yielded requires and warrants no judgment based on the beliefs of the audience of the work. The texture of knowledge extracted, if any is forthcoming, matters not as knowledge, but, like everything else in art, for its formal or sensory effect. Remoteness is all.

This intimation of cognitive disengagement has gone under a variety of titles : Coleridge's "willing suspension of disbelief," Keats's "negative capability," and I. A. Richards's "imaginative assent," all describe a renunciation exacted from the viewer of art of his beliefs in particular and of the process of confirmation in general. Such formulations do not necessarily deny that something like aesthetic inference and denotation as they have been described above figure in the encounter with art; the art work may have implications which *look* like ordinary cognitive assertions. But in accounts of aesthetic distance, the aesthetic attitude toward these implications is radically different from the response ascribed to them in cognitive contexts. We are bound to judge them not as true or false but by other criteria, of consistency or of hypothetical necessity, or (beneath these) of emotive power or suggestion. The viewer of art takes his cues from an order discerned only within the work, not from one which goes outside or beyond it. On these accounts it is not the consequential drive of its reference or representation which enforces the aesthetic experience of an object, but a power which produces a distinctive manner of sensation at at least one remove from any referential context and the viewer's set of beliefs.

The latter point is the most demanding systematic implication of the concept of aesthetic distance; it marks a focus for any critique of that concept and ultimately for the analysis of aesthetic experience more generally. The concept of aesthetic proximity must, then, defer to it. The argument to be followed in showing how this reconciliation can be effected is circuitous, but its conclusions with respect to aesthetic distance are concise enough: namely, that the logical structure of the concept of distance assumes a specious distinction between sensation and reference, between the internal and the external implication of the work of art, items that we hope to find reconciled through the complementary doctrine of aesthetic proximity.

The issue thus opened for discussion is a version of one formulated but unresolved in the preceding chapter: the question of what character the conclusions of aesthetic inference have. The possibility was mentioned that those conclusions do not function in aesthetic experience as do the more usual conclusions of inference. The concept of aesthetic distance has sometimes been taken to imply an even more extreme possibility for such conclusions in the aesthetic moment: that they do not retain the quality of inferential conclusion at all, but are rather transformed by the aesthetic context into nondiscursive, nonimplicative sensations, and sensations alone. But the difficulties of this thesis are clear, and the concept of aesthetic proximity purports to give an alternative account that stops short of the extremity of accounts of aesthetic distance without giving up their attentiveness to the aesthetic side of the encounter with art. What this uncovers is not yet an answer to the "why" of aesthetic experience—but a beginning to that answer.

Aesthetic Proximity. Aesthetic distance and aesthetic proximity are adverbial concepts; they designate aspects of an activity. To distinguish them from each other or to identify them individually is thus to assume a conception of the activity that they qualify and, by implication, a conception of the activities from which that one may be distinguished. It is evident that a single setting may occasion a variety of responses which reflect in turn variety among the criteria or categories applied. We can honorably fail to intervene on behalf of the threatened heroine in a drama, although we cannot do so if the same threats are heard on the street outside the theater. We can use a figurine as a paperweight, evaluating it by criteria of durability and mass; but if we describe it as a good work of art, we refer not to its function in preventing papers from blowing away but to its value in some other service. Shaftesbury provides an early statement concerning the shape of these differences, specifically with respect to aesthetic properties, through his spokesman Theocles:

> Imagine then, good Philocles, if being taken with the beauty of the ocean, which you see yonder at a distance, it should come into your

143

head to seek how to command it, and like some mighty admiral, ride
master of the sea, would not the fancy be a little absurd? [8]

The first attitude cited does not support us in the second. The
objects of the two judgments are identical, at least in one obvious
sense; but the ways in which the object can be regarded are
various. The question of legitimacy as among such contexts of
perception does not arise in the initial distinction: functional in
origin, the differences among them remain bound to a context.

Such general features point to the direction which an
account of the logic of aesthetic proximity, in its relation to
aesthetic distance, will take. The two concepts evidently are
linked both formally and materially: the insulating effect of
aesthetic distance does not imply a total loss of connection;
disinterest should not be confused with uninterest, even if the
two may converge at some final point. Someone uninterested in
everything could hardly avoid being disinterested, even if he
wanted not to be—except of course that he would not. Detachment may thus be detachment from certain aspects of the object
but need not be and probably will not be detachment from all of
them. When one adds to this opening in the concept the evidence
already cited concerning the proximity of the aesthetic moment,
it seems probable that although that moment may imply
detachment from certain contexts or types of activity, the
detachment is balanced by an opposing attachment. The observer must not "take" the aesthetic object in certain ways; but
he will, nonetheless, *take* it. Thus, Bullough, a source for much of
the recent emphasis on the concept of aesthetic distance, defines
the "Antinomy of Distance": "Distance does not imply an
impersonal purely intellectual interested relation. . . . What is
. . . most desirable is the *utmost decrease of distance without its
disappearance.*" [9] There must be at least sufficient attraction or
adhesion for the moment to constitute itself.

To assert this, however, is no more than to offer a glimpse of
the phenomenon, seen now in possession of two facets rather
than one but still revealing nothing of their source and little of
their structure. How are we to understand the unusual conver-

gence of those two vectors, aesthetic distance and aesthetic proximity? Such understanding can come only as we view them in a broader context of action, drawn from categories which apply in other moments of experience as well as in this one. A preliminary point is worth making about the idiom to be employed here in the construction of such a scheme, in particular about the subject-object distinction which it takes for granted. In their empirical no less than in their conceptual order, those terms appear first as bound to each other in a relation and only after that as separable. It is as this sequence has been mistakenly reversed that the phenomenon of bifurcation has occurred in the history of philosophy, concluding with a vision of experience in which either the spectator is irrelevant to what he sees, as on the classical model of Locke's *tabula rasa,* or, as in Berkeley's solipsism, where the perceiver by himself in effect works out of whole cloth the significance of any object and finally the object itself. Neither of these accounts of subject and object, except perhaps as limiting concepts, has much to say about the single context or relation from which they are derived and to which they purportedly answer. For all its normally inconclusive character, the history of philosophy seems, between the two extremities, to have discovered a permanent injunction; this much of the relatedness between subject or object will be taken for granted in the following account.

The varieties of subject-object relation will be designated here as Modes of Articulation, that phase referring to the structure or form of a situation. I mean by "situation" any moment of experience; the Modes of Articulation are applicable, in varying proportions, to all situations or moments. Two Modes of Articulation, that of "Denotation" and that of "Sequence," are central to this analysis. (The question of what other modes there are, or how any of them are derived, is consciously put to one side.) By the Mode of Denotation, I mean the impulse embodied in a moment which refers that moment beyond itself, shaping its identity by its implication of other moments. The form of this mode will be clearer as we consider its appearances. At one end of the spectrum which they mark out is a nexus which is transparent. Here the perceiver looks through or around the objects; he is directed neither beyond it nor even to the object itself. For example: a man walking in a forest comes to a tree lying across the path. His concern is not with the tree, but with a destination which had been set earlier. He may have no concept or term for tree, but only one for destination or the specific place to which he is walking. In the situation described, furthermore, he needs none; certainly he needs it less than he needs one for obstacle. His interest in the tree is limited to the fact that it lies in his way. In observing the tree that blocks the path, the walker's intention is solely to get beyond it; he would not mind, he would not know the difference, if the tree were not there at all; so far as it is there, it is the tree's nonimplicative character that matters, its minimal assertion of itself, the question only of how it can be got around. So far as passivity can characterize an object, not only in perception, but *qua* individual, the tree is passive. One aspect, that of impediment, is attributed to it; the response which that aspect evokes is the question of how best to ignore it. The tree and its other possible aspects count for nothing; the man walks around the tree, and so far as the action of walking toward a destination is concerned, nothing has changed.

Contrast this instance of the Mode of Denotation with that of a similarly constructed situation in which the walker is a botanist. He may have set out with the same purpose as that of the first walker, that is, to reach a destination at the end of the path. But as he comes to the tree lying across the path, he notices the tree itself: that it belongs to a species not previously known in the area, or that it too had died of the common blight, or that its limbs had grown in a peculiar pattern. As any of these possibilities is construed, the quality of the situation (the quality of the mode) alters from what it was for the walker interested only in reaching his destination. The botanist does not look through the tree; his attention is caught by it, and not merely incidentally. The tree asserts itself in his attention (although still not for its own sake), referring the botanist's attention to the class of which it is a member or to a theory in which that class figures. Perhaps at that moment it appears as the beginning or test of a new class or generalization. The situation as implicative is opaque; even if the botanist then walks on, he in effect takes something of the tree along.

It may seem odd that an object like a tree, or, more precisely, the situation of which it is an element, should be said to denote at all. But this follows from the characterization here of its mode, the manner and degree in which a situation refers to some other source. Perception of the tree is not the same for the botanist as it is for the first walker; the difference is founded in what the tree stands for or denotes in his attention.

These two varieties of the Mode of Denotation occupy positions at one of its extremes and at its midpoint; a third point can be anticipated which, as it stands at the other extreme, marks a nexus in which an object is impenetrable—opposed diametrically to that which is transparent. The object stands here at the focus of attention, implicating nothing else, and in this sense, equivalent to the other extreme, but serving in this fashion because it denotes itself so strongly. Examples of this state are not plentiful, if only because it requires an uncommon single-mindedness in the attention of the viewer. Its tendency is much like Blake's vision of "eternity in a grain of sand." One would have to imagine, on the example we have been using, that the walker, coming upon the tree, not only finds his walk interrupted but all consciousness drawn to a focus on the single thing which interrupts it. His awareness goes neither through the object nor around it, but stops with it; even the view of his destination is lost. The stance here, if it is not quite that of the mystic, who may hope to *dissolve* the object, defines a perspective close to his, as that perspective fixes the object and remains poised on it.

The Mode of Sequence represents the temporal conditions that determine a situation, the sequential factors which articulate the moment as process. As distinct from the Mode of Denotation, which is measured by a reference beyond the single situation, moments in the Mode of Sequence establish temporal identity in the situation itself. At one point on the spectrum of this mode is a nexus in which atemporality rules. The drive revealed in situations with such a structure is that of completeness, suggesting as its ideal that the character of the end realized is unchanging or permanent. This would be the Mode of Sequence that applies to scientific judgment or determination, on those conceptions according to which the conclusions of science require no temporal parameter in the formulation: they are meant to endure. At the other extreme of this mode would be the situation in which consideration of change is ordinarily taken for granted. So, for example, the artisan acts to produce an object designed to participate in change. The term "implement" is relational: an implement is *for* an activity. The capacity of the object to act on others is a condition assumed in its production and is the largest single element in the form it assumes.

The median point on the line connecting these alternate Modes of Sequence is the situation in which temporality and atemporality are articulated together. One such situation—I mention it without argument—would be the formulation of an ethical judgment or action. Here, on the one hand, the situation is directed to a point: it is designed to preface, to precede some other situation, not accidentally but essentially. On the other hand, it serves and reflects as a principle which is not itself supposed to change, providing a standard applicable to any future situation which resembles it.

I suggest that these Modes of Denotation and Sequence, taken together, provide a useful means for organizing and understanding certain patterns in the contours of experience. They serve as a key to a map, underscoring the fact that the map coming to view without such a key would hardly count as a map at all. Ideally, no feature of the map would remain unaccounted for in the reckoning of such modes; how fully the two modes cited realize this, and whether additions to them would provide a more useful or purposeful rendering of the map, can be determined only as applications of the modes are made; I claim only that certain characteristic moments of experience are explicable in terms of the two modes and that one of them is the moment on which the vectors of aesthetic distance and aesthetic proximity converge.

Consider, as a means of locating by contrast this "aesthetic" convergence, the intersection of the Modes of Denotation and Sequence, which might be called the theoretical moment. In its paradigm form, this moment identifies the act of scientific or mathematical conceptualization: in one sense, the denotative relation from a particular object to a general scheme based on it (as, for example, in the case of the botanist); in another sense, the drive, coordinated with that of the first mode, for atemporality— that the structure realized be permanent. The instrumental moment represents a convergence of the two modes of simple process (in the Mode of Sequence) and transparency (in the Mode of Denotation). The character of its object reflects a design for future use; in the Mode of Denotation, we find that the object which serves as a means beyond itself in itself is transparent: there is no reason for dwelling on it. What is primary in its structure is what it leads to. If one's purpose is to get to Chicago from New York, the means by which the journey is made is something only to be left behind.

Nine principal moments of convergence and an indefinite number of intermediate ones are functions of the two modes described. These intersections mark some of the important loci of experience; we can distinguish through their applications, for example, among crafting or making, sensual experience like tasting or feeling, religious practice. A more complete rendering than is attempted here would show the articulation of each of such convergences, as well as how the moments themselves are initially disclosed. But my principal concern is with the aesthetic moment and how, on the scheme outlined, the phenomena of distance and proximity are accounted for. What we have found among the conditions of the work of art prior to this, specifically its denotative possibilities, provides a natural opening to the Modes of Articulation. Applying the Mode of Denotation to the reflective judgment which is the source of those possibilities, we discover that in it the object is neither transparent nor impenetrable. In one way the judgment reflects the object as it is itself realized in light of the object; yet there also emerges from the moment the denial of its impenetrability, an impulse of judgment driving beyond the object to something which, if not simply different from it, is yet more than it is. Thus, for the Mode of Denotation in the aesthetic moment we locate a midpoint between transparency and opacity, what can be named translucence. The situation has denotative force, not in the way that the theoretical moment does, but as it exhibits what it denotes. It reaches beyond the immediate given, but only in terms provided by that given. (This is, it will be noted, a variant form of denotation which answers to the requirements set in chapter 3 in the discussion of the heresy of paraphrase.)

For the Mode of Sequence, the juxtaposition of aesthetic proximity and distance sets one principal condition: the viewer somehow takes the object. This condition eliminates the possibility that the quality of that juxtaposition will be one of permanence, which is a feature, in this mode, of theoretical judgment; it also argues against mere seriality which would render the moment isolated, discrete, and devoid of persistence. The conclusion of the aesthetic moment is located between these two points: it results in a process, something happening and continuing to, and yet it is not the process alone which is asserted. It appears designed to persist; so, perhaps, a label analogous to translucence is needed: persistence—and not simply as a means.

Although the balance between aesthetic distance and proximity is at stake in the intersection of these modes, the emphasis on them varies. Aesthetic distance is emphasized in its appearance in the Mode of Denotation, in which judgment operates to an end which is general, detached—the art work's summoning up something which is not, in the art work, an object already present. Aesthetic proximity, although acknowledged in that end, becomes a more prominent feature in the Mode of Sequence, as the viewer is involved both in and beyond the presence of the art work. Thus, the constrained assertive or theoretical character evident in the Mode of Denotation for the aesthetic moment is found to differ even further from the reference of the theoretical moment by its ingression in a process in the Mode of Sequence. This account answers the requirements urged in chapter 3, in light of the heresy of paraphrase, for a means of retaining the concept of aesthetic inference without yet reducing it to inference *simpliciter.* The peculiar characteristics of denotation as it was presented there are seen now to pertain to one aspect or moment in the more inclusive Mode of Denotation.

The Aesthetic Proximity of Belief. This account, even if it accomplishes everything it purports to, is still fixing an apparatus, locating a moment; it is not an explanation. But in doing that much, it discloses a pattern in certain phenomenal features of art—if not a necessary at least an important condition for their explanation. The question remains as to why art acts in the way described; but that question could have no force if the way itself were not acknowledged. It is necessary before addressing that issue to return to the initial question raised in this chapter: namely, what the role of the viewer is in the aesthetic moment described. The Modes of Articulation define that role formally and externally. But finally, of course, the appearances they comprehend have an inside as well as an outside, and it is on the former that analysis of the status of belief in the aesthetic moment bears.

Two principal questions govern the issue of the relation between art and belief: first, whether it makes sense to speak of the engagement of belief as part of the aesthetic moment, and second, assuming an affirmative answer to the first, whether the beliefs so involved differ in any way from beliefs engaged in other situations, from other sources. Certain preliminary comments point the way. One of these is tautologous and not very illuminating: that the force of aesthetic experience implies *some* connection between perceiver and object. This does not mean that belief is the form which the connection takes, but it does mean that whatever we claim to be involved in the connection cannot be excluded on the grounds that there is no adhesion to the perceiver.

A more substantial qualification is based on the consequences which would follow if we rule out any role for belief. Those consequences are plain and sharp: if the viewer's beliefs in no way matter to the experience, then it also does not matter what they are or even that they are. If the suspension of disbelief stands by itself as a condition of aesthetic experience, it can be met, one supposes, by a viewer innocent of any beliefs or one who held a large number of very odd beliefs, as well as by anyone else; the viewer who brings no context of belief to bear will be in no different a position with respect to the work of art (perhaps even in an advantageous one) than the perceiver who has beliefs and is asked to put them aside. Thus, the viewer who has never reflected on the moral consequences of the act of murder will be as responsive to a performance of Euripides' *Medea* as the spectator who has done so but has disengaged himself: the point in both cases is that his beliefs should not matter.

This line of analysis, however, has little to recommend it. Admittedly, to deny its extremity leaves open the possibility of various levels at which belief may be said to be pertinent; but it is important first to note the implications of ruling out that possibility as a whole. And it is difficult, even if one were able to find a viewer who had made no prior assessment of murder or one who could at will disengage himself from that assessment, to see why or how that condition would add to his appreciation of *Medea* or even allow it. To argue that this should be the case flies in the face of the response which has been a fact. That evidence may eventually be asked to give way by a higher level abstraction, but the sheer bulk of what would thus have to be explained away itself constitutes an objection to such removal.

This point recurs as we distinguish among the levels at which belief may impinge in the encounter with art. Two of these levels, in particular, are germane: the first, of beliefs which are general conditions for understanding; the second, of beliefs which figure in the distinctively aesthetic context. The relevance of the first of these is obvious, and most versions even of the thesis which rejects the role of belief in aesthetic experience acknowledge it, although without accepting its implications. Coleridge's phrase, again, is the "willing suspension of disbelief," suggesting not that beliefs which conflict should not be beliefs, but only that they should not obtrude. There is no reason to attach to this the a priori rider, which is logically compatible with it, that in viewing the work of art, we ought to blot out all beliefs and cognitive commitments—to set aside, for instance, our understanding that men walk on their feet, that the meanings of words are not limitless, etc. There will be, in other terms, an undercurrent of belief, of dispositions to see and understand in certain ways, which any viewer of art, simply as a sentient being, will carry about with him whatever the circumstances. It seems incontrovertible that those beliefs will figure, furthermore, in the encounter with art. The artist presupposes them not only as it happens; it is difficult to know what he could do if he were not able to take them for granted.[10]

The infringement of belief in this manner is of no special significance for art except insofar as it refutes the extreme position noted above. It no more specifically pertains to the encounter with art than it does to any other activity—hanging a picture on the wall or eating dinner. And even if the wedge it provides becomes a significant opening, there is no reason to suspect it at this point. Or there would be no reason if this were the whole of the matter, which it is not. For if we return to the conclusions of reflective judgment which, on the reckoning of criticism, assume so preeminent a role in the articulation of the work of art, not only are beliefs presupposed as a prior condition of our grasping what the work is, but others are engaged at the conclusion of that process. The conclusions of aesthetic inference, governing not primarily the first sight of the work of art but the view of it as a whole, have the shape of representations which invite assent. Those conclusions usually stand at the crux of discussions of the way in which belief figures in the aesthetic moment; it is here that the claims for the irrelevance of belief to the aesthetic moment refer to disengagement or imaginative assent, or in the present discussion disinterest and distance. Perhaps, so the arguments run, in some ancillary sense beliefs are engaged in the aesthetic moment; but finally, in the large results to which art reaches, they are put aside. After all of the preliminary practical beliefs have been assimilated, the others do not matter. It is a matter of indifference, for example, so far as concerns the import or value of Dickinson's poem, whether "the truly significant things in human experience" really "dwell in the realm of silence," or not.

This alleged irrelevance of belief is taken in such accounts to be a characteristic difference between the aesthetic moment and other moments in which an identically formulated conclusion may emerge. If a psychoanalyst made the statement inferred from Dickinson's poem to a patient, for example, its truth would be assuredly a matter of importance; for art, however, evaluative criteria do not include this feature. Art may indeed turn out to engender proposals of a covert metaphysics, but in art, as distinct from other means of expression, the truth or falsity of the assertions carries no weight. To regard art otherwise is to infringe on its integrity, in effect, to mis-take it.

This claim, like the one argued here against it, is not merely descriptive. Some viewers of art obviously do judge it in terms of its convergence on their beliefs; if not, the issue would hardly arise. The opposing contention must hold, then, that something characteristic and valuable in art will be threatened by the imposition of such criteria, and conversely, that something distinctively germane to art is realized by addressing it on the grounds of belief. The systematic implications which have been cited weigh heavily on the side of the latter claims. As we have seen, the form of the process at work in aesthetic experience resembles in significant ways forms which have slight aesthetic importance, as, for instance, the process of derivation in a theory of science. The sole criterion for distinguishing works of art from each other and from other objects, if this isomorphism is consistently asserted, is exclusively a matter of formal complexity and relation; and even a superficial consideration of this consequence reveals the difficulties in it. Furthermore, as the weaker version of this thesis admits the relevance of certain elementary practical applications of belief, the question gains strength of whether the covenant protecting those elementary applications may not extend to larger aspects of the work of art as well.

Such considerations are reinforced by the conclusions of the analysis of the Modes of Articulation. In that analysis the emergence of reflective judgment is not moved by a theoretical impulse, which would be content to leave the judgment alone, once realized, but by a connective element acting in such a way that the viewer places himself within the process and its conclusion. This feature, it should be noted, has been anticipated earlier in our discussion, in both the performative character ascribed to reflective judgment (where the critic, by his act, brings the judgment to life), and in the expansive force attributed to aesthetic denotation. We seemingly have here a convergence of descriptions that may not be quite independent of each other but are sufficiently diverse to reinforce each other.

What is intimated in this convergence is that reflective judgment attaches to itself the "I" of the viewer by way of an assent on his part. That assent is not a dislocation from his other commitments, although it may enlarge on them. Its divergence from them is not substantive but formal: it is the assent itself, the distinctive character of the performance, not some consequent feature like understanding or usefulness, which engages the "I" of the viewer. As the generalizing move of reflective judgment expands the latter's denotation to include this "I," the observer is bound to the particularity and presence of the art work. He finds himself involved in its exhibitive properties. It does not describe or imply for him as an object detached, as an abstract or impersonal thing. He is absorbed by the dialectic it establishes, through the Modes of Articulation, between the actual and the possible—a tension which is enlarged as the work involves the detail of his actuality and his possibility.

This occurrence invokes something more than the minimal and circumstantial elements of belief referred to previously under the weak thesis of belief in art. So far as the viewer is engaged by the work, in the absence of a specific exclusionary principle, the totality of his commitments as a subject will be open to the moment. Some of them may later be excluded as irrelevant or false, on the basis of detail in the particular moment, but not in any event on a priori grounds. The viewer is limited in his acknowledgement of the confirmations opened to him in the work only by the character of the self, most immediately, of course, by his own; remotely, of the self in its capacities and impulses as self. The elements which appear through the filter of the art work might matter to the observer if he encountered them in abstract form no more than would any extra-aesthetic objects or moments; he attends to them aesthetically for distinctive reasons: not that they hold in general, or have held in fact for someone in particular, but because they represent the turning of a particular present (his) into a particular future, under the reflection of a general and animating principle. Through the intercession of the artist, he is enabled to see and to experience further—enlarging both on vision and existence—than he would by himself; but he cannot do this unless he takes the self being enlarged—his past—along. In opening himself to the episodes of an "aesthetic education," the observer seeks coherence between the art work and what he has conceived to be true and (in some measure because of this) to be important; he addresses a possibility posed by the work in response to an inquiry pointed by what he has been and has believed. In seizing on that possibility, he opens himself to a confirmation of the self, gaining from that encounter a representation of himself in a texture of actual and possible experience. The clarification realized by this representation both affects the strands of experience past and, as they open the past to him in the present, invokes the prospect of novelty. It is a turning which summons him, or as much of him as a given work is able to evoke. As outside of art he is concerned to establish the terms of experience on a foundation which is at once rich and coherent, it is no incongruity that he should seek similar terms even in the distinctive working of art or that art, in the drive which sponsors it, should provide them.

The implications of this account extend to the important question left from the preceding chapter as to the generality of denotation in reflective judgment. That generality, it turns out, includes certain peculiar features. For one thing, what is denoted includes aspects of the "I," the critic or viewer, who becomes aware of the denotation. For another, that "I," which is responsible for the process by which the work is addressed, is itself also within the process. The art work does not then denote concepts or qualities which are complete and transparent independently of the work (this is the usual and simplest form ascribed to denotation), but concepts or qualities or activities which are as much prospective as factual, and not only historical or theoretical, but personal. The process quite literally involves a "finding" of the self, both in the sense that to do this implies the existence of a self to be found—and that the finding will alter that existence.

The generality of denotation, indeed, the very phenomenon of denotation, seemed in the discussion in chapter 3 to hold less readily for some arts than for others. I proposed, in acknowledging this qualification, that if what has been said about denotation did apply to the arts in general, we should be able to determine that this was the case by examining the instances where its applicability was least at issue and by then analyzing the form of its application to the other appearances of art. The concept of belief provides a means for the latter task. There is little basis for assuming that arts as diverse as architecture and the dance, literature and music, conspire to a single material end; it would be more than just a surprise if they, or each of their instances, "said" the same thing, yielded identical reflective judgments. But it is possible nonetheless to see each of them utilizing its own respective material to fit a common form, retrieving for their audiences an inchoate structure of experience and sending them out to follow its implication. The form of reflective judgment, in other words, may be constant, and the arts could realize this common end if they together engaged their audience in something like the process of belief described here. That they do this in fact will be the burden of the argument in chapter 5.

The Aesthetic Proximity of Belief. This conception of the role of belief does not mean that the art work may not clash with the commitments or expectations of its audience, or that it cannot enlarge upon them; it means that if the observer takes the work of art seriously, he takes it seriously as a live and important possibility—a *true* possibility for himself. The writers who affirm one version or another of the aesthetic doctrine of the suspension of disbelief, understanding by this that the world conjured in art is merely possible as distinguished from the actual world of beliefs, leave untouched one important question. For unless they assert that any possibility offered in the art work will, as possible, command the same intensity of attention as any other, they must distinguish among the "possible" possibilities. And, contrary to this, it is clear that the art work, in its hold on an audience, does not introduce any or a mere possibility of experience, but a possibility which for good reason establishes itself in the grasp of its viewer. The latter may have no prior criteria for assessing the validity of that possibility, but even so, an evolving criterion will apply which the viewer himself provides of how the new experience coheres with or puts a point to or expands beyond (and possibly all three) his previous experience.

It should be noticed that this argument does not claim that because art is important to man, a commitment is therefore entailed on his part; or that so far as belief is a factor in aesthetic experience, the experience is the more important to him. Many activities engage him that only remotely bear on such beliefs. Where, in the case of art, commitment or belief is an integral element, this occurs not because of a decision beforehand that it should do so, but because art itself confirms the fact. Although the discovery of the power of art may at first come as a surprise, there is nothing gratuitous about that discovery; but there is nothing premeditated about it, either. Art may have had an instrumental origin, as most writers on its early history contend. But this does not imply that art continues to exist for the same reason. Its sustained importance seems rather to be linked to the viewer's willingness to give assent to those of its elements which impinge on his experience. Regardless of whether those elements are defined as distinctively aesthetic or as reducible to other, nonaesthetic terms, his response is inexplicable without the acknowledgment of that assent.

The quality of belief as it has been described may seem exceptional. Belief is often represented by the interested believer as a disinterested activity, responding to truths which are quite independent of any attitudes toward it. Beliefs in certain contexts undoubtedly have this character; I suggest, however, that belief in the context of art assumes a different form, one which converges on the "performative" character of reflective judgment and which may itself be called by that name. In it, the viewer is not negotiating with facts as one who is himself complete and independent of them; his view of the work and what it opens to him actually contributes to what he then is. The affirmation he gives to the work or its aspects amounts to an affirmation of aspects which he had previously not known or realized, or even which, in a strict sense, did not exist. If we think of his commitment as performative, a doing, a "belief in" rather than a "belief that," we come closest to its status vis-à-vis the more common variety of belief.

This manner of involvement poses a danger in the emergence of aesthetic experience analogous to the danger in accounts which exaggerate the force of aesthetic distance. As the latter define a moment of experience which verges on the theoretical process of generalization, finding and leaving the viewer *personally* quite unmoved, so the former might be understood to reduce the experience to the mere particularity of historical events and qualities. Such a reduction is exemplified in the loss of distance on which melodrama and soap opera thrive. In these cases the observer not only finds himself committed to the immediate detail of the work, but he finds no more than such detail in it—regarding the moment not as a synthesis or dialectic of the possible and the actual, of the general and the particular, but only as an actual and particular present. He treats the work in effect as history. The tears he sheds are shed for the same reasons he sheds them in moments having nothing to do with art; he becomes the spectator who leaps onto the stage to defend the honor of the threatened heroine.

This possibility, however, like the other, does not impugn the account. The issue is not whether such a response is possible: people do, of course, respond in this way. Like its alternate extreme, however, the consequence of underdistancing or of assuming the exclusive relevance of aesthetic proximity is that

159

the existence of art, as we distinguish it from the process of ordinary experience, is quite simply and flatly denied.

The properties attributed to the art work by way of the concept of proximity do not require that interest in the work be guided by the test of whether it is simply true or false, even in the attenuated sense of those terms which has been indicated. Works of art are ordinarily so complex that their totality, measured by this criterion, will be equivocal, although one can imagine at the extremes works which are either so fundamentally specious or so overwhelmingly persuasive as to preclude reservations. More commonly, however, such a decisive judgment will not be possible. This fact does not mean that appreciation of the work will necessarily be obstructed, but that the process is complicated and that the final judgment represents a balance. The medieval Catholic world view which stands at the foundation of the *Divine Comedy*, for example, may be criticized by a reader because, for example, it invokes the premise of divine reward and punishment. But the same reader may judge that other elements in the work, such as the sense it affords of the profusion of evil, overbalance this first defect; or that the objectionable thesis itself can be understood in terms suggested internally as, for example, a parable of the destructiveness of evil.

The pattern in the appearances of aesthetic proximity reflects the pertinence of two formal criteria which, surely by something more than accident, resemble the so-called coherence and the correspondence accounts of truth. The former of these criteria requires internal consistency, that the girl who is tall on one page of the novel should not be short on a later one (unless she lives in Alice's Wonderland, where it would be inconsistent if this were not the case). Larger examples of the same principle would be the development of a character in a novel, or the balance in a painting. In its most comprehensive form, the principle reflects on the style of a work; the very concept of style presupposes the recognition of such consistency.

The pertinence of this internal coherence as a criterion brings to light a second and logically prior criterion of correspondence between elements in the work and others external to it. For if coherence within a system is deemed a virtue, we may still ask, from outside the system, why this is the case. The answer suggested by the concept of aesthetic proximity invokes a larger coherence, or correspondence, between the art work and the broad span of experience in which it comes to hold a place. The thesis that the beliefs of the audience are engaged in the encounter with art as it catches the attention of the viewer provides an explanation of the importance of internal coherence; there is nothing surprising about the latter if a similar demand for coherence underlies it at a more fundamental level still. This does not mean that the work of art may not include tension or irony among its elements. It implies only, and it seems thus to answer to what the spectator asks, that there should be a consistency between whatever it is that art affirms, including its ambiguities and disharmonies, and the elements of experience to which the viewer contrives to fit it. Thus, at least in part, comes the inspiration of Plato's statement in the *Phaedrus* that "a fair speech can be made in defense of a false thesis; but the greatest speech will be that which defends a true one."

The assertion of the relevance of belief to aesthetic experience faces a last and serious problem insofar as it suggests that there may be no limits to the extent of the aesthetic moment. If belief figures in the relation between the audience and the work, and if the relation has the power to make that belief explicit and significant, then what is presented in the work may linger indefinitely, or as long as the beliefs or their consequences endure. It may seem, then, that we should have, for example, to include the suicides which occurred in the aftermath of the publication of Goethe's *Young Werther* as a manner of the aesthetic response to that work.[11] Two considerations previously anticipated bear on this objection. For one, it should be noted that the issue at stake, although underscored in connection with the cognitive conception of art, is not restricted to it. Even a rigorously formalistic account of art which would take exception to much that has been asserted here faces the question of what the relation is between memories of aesthetic form and its direct appreciation, of how the spread of those effects is to be construed in aesthetic terms. The phenomenology of our discussion, in its distinguishing among types of activity, suggests a means of limiting the question. The readers who acted on their reading of *Werther* were doing precisely that—involving their response in a decision beyond the response itself. In other words, the aesthetic moment, construed here as marking a boundary between the actual present and a domain of possibility, was involved by them in a decision which rendered the balance between the possible and the actual actual alone. To an extent the aesthetic moment figures in the latter process, but that is to say no more than that nothing in experience ever disappears without a trace. What is crucial is that in the action taken, the initial modality of the aesthetic moment is superseded by a different modality. The difference is not that the one is a doing, the other not; the aesthetic moment, too, I have claimed, is a form of *praxis* with at least something of the productive quality which such activity ever has. But there is a difference in the doing, principally in the role of the doer and in the absence of any decision from the aesthetic moment. The viewer does not decide on the comprehension or affirmation which the art work provides any more than he decides to see the validity of a mathematical theorem. This does not mean, either, that the viewer of art is passive or that what alters is some intangible internal state in him, a ghost in the machine. What changes in the recognition of art's claims, I am suggesting, is a disposition of the self which defines a condition for particular actions; it is separable from the latter logically and for the self, personally.

The Final Cause of Aesthetic Proximity. In discussing the relevance of belief to aesthetic experience, I have not faced the issue of how aesthetic proximity obtains its adhesive power— why, in more general terms, the drive for aesthetic experience occurs at all. That question must be confronted if the other facts of the matter are to have more than impressionistic value; it constitutes what I take to be the final question to which aesthetics as an enterprise turns—the question that supplies to the other questions of aesthetics whatever substance they have.

Put concisely, it asks what in the work of art, on the one hand, and in human nature, on the other, makes the experience (formalized now in the categories of aesthetic proximity) possible.

Analogous questions and answers are readily apparent for other modes of analysis. One, for example, is Aristotle's referral of the lure of the theoretical structure of mathematics to the drive of reason for an immutable object. I do no more for the moment than hint at an answer to the same question as it concerns aesthetic experience. The epigraphs at the beginning of the chapter are pertinent here, and two other quotations may be appended. One is Spinoza's statement in the *Ethics* that "No one can desire to be blessed, to act rightly, and to live rightly, without at the same time wishing to be, to act, and to live." (pt. 4, Prop. 21); the second is from Valéry, as he speaks about the work of the poet as "le travail qui fait vivre en nous ce qui n'existe pas." What is striking about the terms of aesthetic proximity is that the dialectic between the potential and the actual defined there seems to join elements drawn from immediately recognizable and fundamental forms of experience—on the one side, a world of general possibility; on the other, men as subject, fixed on practical and isolated and actual matters of fact. The one offers him the allure of permanence, universality, mastery; the other, the conditions of individual existence, contingent and indeterminate. Aesthetic experience, I shall argue in greater detail, heightens for the participant the force that this dialectic retains in even common experience; in doing so, it yields the sense which perhaps more than any other dominates aesthetic experience, that one is somehow, having gone through it, more than he had been. Man is not himself a general principle, but he knows that and knows how such principles apply to his situation; he is not a gross particular, an object, but he cannot escape the constraints which link him with them. The aesthetic experience joins these conditions of experience; in facing them, the individual concretely realizes what that individuality entails, and perhaps not so much discovers this, as creates it. The commitment to present fact and future possibility, reflecting the convergence of the particular and the general, govern that effort. Thus, if it can be further shown, the ambience of belief in the sources and ends of art.

Notice that at no point in this discussion has the question been whether beliefs *do* enter into any particular response to art. This is an empirical issue alone, and it is possible, then, that belief should not be so involved. Nor has the question discussed been whether the art work as art work *should* elicit a response of the kind described: this would, even denying the conclusions reached here, no more than invoke the larger question of whether art should exist at all, or, finally, of whether man should be man. What I have been considering is the question of whether a speculative basis can be found to account for a body of prima facie evidence, a thread which runs through a large number of the appearances of what is commonly designated to be art and the response of the audience to it. The question of whether other, surer, possibilities of explanation obtain must return to the evidence itself, in the arts and in the process of their articulation.

The Work in Process

When all the other questions have been directed to the appearances of art, about the forms of criticism and appreciation, about the power of its quality and denotation, one yet remains which (more simply) questions its existence: *"Why Art rather than non-Art?" That inquiry is an evident parody of one better known, more fundamental than it (or any other), on the uneasy balance between Being and non-Being. A procedural analogy, furthermore, links the two questions: either would be more easily handled, perhaps they could only be answered, as we move beyond the alternatives, to locate an independent point from which the terms contrasted may be viewed. Beyond Being and non-Being little space remains: thus, the boundary condition of the question itself. For Art, however, there exists a mitigated possibility: "possibility," because not everything in experience is (or is equally) art; "mitigated," because the distinction applies in some measure to all the objects or processes of experience. To color the many shades of Art and non-Art is to leave no room over on the spectrum.*

The means for working this possibility are correspondingly limited. One—already used—follows the contrast from without; a schematism of the kinds and grades of the aesthetic moment against those which it is not—*how it is like them (or not). One other remains—concerning the contrasts asserted from* within *the aesthetic moment. For unless we say (as it has sometimes been said) that all art is equally and only that (i.e., Art), we may yet find inside it a variable structure in the shadings of which the form of art as a whole is made intelligible. Then, if we can keep*

165

the two approaches on art as separate as its outside from its inside, there will be comfort in their convergence (if they do)—and righteous confusion, if they don't.

However such process advances, the last question of aesthetics yet persists and, if anything, is enlarged by the advance: "Why, after all, art? Why?" In the face of that radical question, our instinct may be to retreat, midst a number of covering stratagems. We could, for example, hoping to discredit the question, stop short with the phenomenon; after all, we have to stop someplace. But surely—since we otherwise ask (and find answers to) questions that begin with "Why?"—we cannot afford to stop on the authority of the "high priori." And surely if we are to find substantial grounds for stopping or proceeding, we must first see what would count as an answer; but to do this requires that we at least provisionally admit the question itself.

Or again, we might first admit the question—and then hope to turn it aside: " 'Why Art?' you ask. Well, there's a human need for it." ("Otherwise, why would it exist?") But of the making of tautologies there is no end, and, even at the end, small profit. What we could achieve along this way is no particular explanation, but a formal conclusion to fit any explanation whatsoever, thus leaving it something less than conclusive.

This is not to say that answers which end in an appeal to human nature should never be begun—but only that before we admit them, we must have shown that there is no other place to go; and that analogously located places—the other sides of man's nature—are not more fundamental than this one. The ghost of such appeals is a constant guest at the feasts philosophy sets. The substance of the response to those appeals is open to change, and to appeal, both with the uncovering of new objects—this, in the instance at hand, through the possibility of innovation in art—and because of the tentativeness of concepts (such as the concept of art): this, through the various future open to thought.

We cannot hope, as the "Why's?" asked about the data of experience respond to fewer and more general strands of that experience, to see as immediately or concretely as we do early in the inquiry. Such diminution increases not because answers to the later questions have no empirical contact, but because, as they sweep more comprehensively towards the perimeter of experience, they unavoidably become themselves less visible, less explicit. If the options of conceptualization are broader than the options of sight, that freedom is, on the obverse side, an abstraction or separation from fact.

A final point reinforces the challenge of an already sharp question. In speaking (provisionally) of art, we recognize that art itself is provisional. In asking "Why Art, rather than non-Art?" we recognize, by history's own testimony that art indeed may (or may sometime) not be. Contingencies, then, lurk not only in the prospect of an answer to the question, but qualify the question as question. They are not, however, mere liabilities. In an inquiry open in so many ways, they comprise one of the few constraints giving shape to the answer: we may reasonably hope to discern what art itself embodies by the light of what is not (or less) art. Here, too, as in the venture toward art from its exterior, we reach for the tenuous end at which philosophical inquiry and fact, in their last resorts, meet.

. . . Were we to play a trick on our lover of the beautiful, and plant in the ground artificial flowers (which can be made so as to look like natural ones), and perch artfully carved birds on the branches of trees, and he were to find out how he had been taken in, the immediate interest which these things previously had for him would at once vanish. . . .

Kant, Critique of Aesthetic Judgment

Suppose . . . that a finely wrought object, one whose texture and proportions are highly pleasing in perception, has been believed to be a product of some primitive people. Then there is discovered evidence that proves it to be an accidental natural product. As an external thing, it is now precisely what it was before. Yet at once it ceases to be a work of art and becomes a natural "curiosity." It now belongs in a museum of natural history, not in a museum of art.

Dewey, Art as Experience

"If a man hacking in fury at a block of wood," Stephen continued, "make there an image of a cow, is that image a work of art? If not, why not?"

"That's a lovely one," said Lynch. . . . "That has the true scholastic stink."

Joyce, Portrait of the Artist
as a Young Man

5

Intentionality
and the Ontology of Art

That moments differ in the measure of their aesthetic promise or significance is an innocuous assertion to appear at a late point in this discussion which has repeatedly implied it. Yet it is important to consider the claim explicitly and on its own grounds: the ontology of art (as distinct, for example, from the analysis of criticism) *affirms* the fact of art itself. Recognition of this need shapes the question raised in this chapter which asks finally and most generally how the aesthetic moment, its features having been located first in the language of criticism and then in certain more abstract appearances, is itself possible.

This question openly assumes the delineation of an aesthetic texture, and thus a distinction between that texture and others. I have already indicated (see chapter 1) why such a claim is unavoidably ad hoc, why it cannot itself be demonstrated: unless one could independently show both that reality has joints ready for the carving and that the carver can be certain of the location of those joints, this ad hoc status is unavoidable. This qualification holds, in fact, for the discrimination of any type or mode of experience, and the force behind it is disclosed in the whole of the preceding discussion: the analysis extending from art criticism to aesthetic proximity pointed to art as a fact, but the evidence, so far as concerns the conceptual distinction, remains no more than circumstantial. This is not an excuse, then, for unclarity or indecisiveness in the account; it asserts that those features are intrinsic to it.

In contrast, there is an obvious difference between mere possibility and the probability which the following discussion ascribes to the aesthetic texture. The basis of that ascription has already been indicated. The language and intention of criticism, the features of denotation and proximity, point overtly if not unmistakably to a distinctive mode of experience. The echoes of that distinction, furthermore, grow stronger as we consult the prima facie and less systematic evidence. If, for example, there were no grounds for distinguishing aesthetic (in some sense) from nonaesthetic quality, we could expect to find no differences in the aesthetic potentialities of various objects or moments. All moments would be of equal aesthetic relevance or irrelevance; and it would follow from this in turn that neither the viewer nor the object of his experience contributes differentially to its then nondiscriminable aesthetic quality: that any viewer and any object equal every other in their respective potentials for aesthetic experience. But these consequences provide a strong prima facie argument against the premises, on grounds independent of any so far cited. Following them, we should expect the patient squirming on a dentist's chair to be able to appreciate the Titian hanging on the wall no differently than if he faced it in any other setting; or a reader—even the "ideal" reader—to find no significant difference in aesthetic quality between *War and Peace* and the Manhattan telephone directory. Such examples can be easily multiplied; surely they render suspect the premises that produce them.

This reductio argument may seem only to beg the question. It has no edge against the objection that there is in fact no aesthetic difference between *War and Peace* and the telephone directory; it begs the question even before this as it selects the examples of the Titian and of *War and Peace* out of an at that point indefinitely large range of objects. But if its procedure is in some way circular, it has the important advantage of circling around a center defined by common usage and sense.

The epigraphs from Kant and Dewey at the beginning of this chapter provide a more sophisticated but related statement of the evidence on which this reductio is based. They suggest not only that different objects or moments vary in aesthetic force, but that the aesthetic relation between even a single object and a single viewer, following changes in either of those foci, will also change. The plausible shifts in experience described in the epigraphs are comprehensible only as we posit a variable potential in the individual object and the individual viewer. The experience about which Kant and Dewey report, then, attests to the responsibility of elements within the particular aesthetic context for making the art work appear when it does and for altering its appearance when that happens. Stephen Daedelus's question would have no point—or "stink"—if it were not evident that for specific instances other than the one he refers to, a line between the work of art and the nonwork or lesser work of art was indeed visible.

Again, although this claim is superficially innocuous, it is conceptually weighty and has been postponed in the previous argument precisely because of its scope. To establish the distinction between the aesthetic and the nonaesthetic may not be the obligation of aesthetic inquiry alone or even primarily; it is difficult to know where the responsibility for actually dispensing experience resides, but it is unlikely to be exclusively in the conclusions or aspirations of philosophy. But neither can the end that philosophy hopes to reach be realized independently of the story which "mere" experience tells. The statements of Kant and Dewey are pertinent to the analysis of the character of art precisely because they are so unexceptionable as reflections on the surface of art: there can be no disputing the possibility of the shifting qualities of experience that those statements describe. I shall attempt to show that, in reflecting on that surface, the statements point to certain ontological features of art which underlie the appearances of art related in the three preceding chapters.

The Evidence of Intentionality. Each of the epigraphs at the beginning of this chapter, attesting to the difference between an aesthetic and non (or less) aesthetic moment, involves a single object and a single viewer. The changes described in the quality

171

of the moment explicated are due, furthermore, not to a flaw or idiosyncrasy in either side of the relation (the examples would have no force if that were their point) but to a predictable functional pattern. The occasion described by Kant is determined not by the specific aesthetic or nonaesthetic properties of natural or artificial flowers, any more than Dewey's example is tied to a single "finely wrought object": any natural objects might substitute for Kant's example, and a corresponding range, Dewey indicates on the other side, is possible for the class of artifacts. The substantive implication of the point thus made requires little arguing beyond the examples themselves: there would be common agreement, I take it, that to have appraised what was taken to be an actual sunset as a "third-rate Turner" and then to find out that it *is* a Turner will argue for a revision in the original judgment; or that if generations of monkeys hopping around on typewriters turned out to have written not only all the books already in the British Museum but some new ones as well, surely a question would be raised about the status of those later works (together perhaps with one about the status of the monkeys[1]).

The classes of objects represented in the statements of Dewey and Kant, furthermore, are exhaustive. They refer to artifacts, on the one hand, and to natural entities, on the other; and if those classes are viewed in their fullest extent, nothing is omitted from their combined membership to which distinctive qualities, aesthetic or nonaesthetic, can be ascribed. The examples represent the entire range of possible objects.

Still unspecified in any of these comments are the aesthetic (or nonaesthetic) features of either natural phenomena or artifacts. Neither Kant nor Dewey in the passages cited stipulates what those properties are, although they do so elsewhere, partly in response to the passages themselves. What is of primary importance in the passages is the suggestion that the significant differences in aesthetic quality between natural and "artful" objects may be explicable in terms of a single categorial relation; in other words, that variations of aesthetic quality—and if those variations are echoed within each of the classes of aesthetic and nonaesthetic objects, there too—can be accounted for by a single feature of the context in which the objects appear. There is the implication in this claim that all objects are potential aesthetic objects, and I shall attempt to make clear the sense in which this is the case; for the moment it is worth noting only that this consequence would be consistent with the assertion of differences (they could be of degree, not necessarily of kind) in the aesthetic relevance of objects.

In following the instances cited by Kant and Dewey, we shall be obliged to go beyond them, beyond even the systematic accounts otherwise provided by Kant and Dewey. But the two statements point towards a formal explanation as they indicate that the aesthetic moment (whether involving natural or artificial objects) is functional or contextual in character; it turns not on a simple aesthetic property, but on a relation among the elements which constitute the moment. If the relational variable that is responsible for this contextual shift can be identified, we will have gone some distance toward understanding the character of the aesthetic moment. One variable in particular can be abstracted from the instances cited. Both of those instances reveal a shift in the expectation which the viewer brings to the objects, specifically in the reversal which such expectation undergoes. The viewer in each case discovers that his predisposition towards a particular object requires revision; the change which this discovery effects makes a significant difference (one might say *all* the difference) in his appreciation of the object. The sources of that expectation at any point in its history are less pertinent immediately than is its status as a function of a relational order. The latter feature is of special importance to the understanding of the way in which art exerts its force; but this importance will become evident only as the elements of expectation are identified.

Three principal components distinguish the phenomenon of expectation: (a) the process is directed towards an object whose character affects the form of the process (if we expect rain, we dress differently, or decide not to, than we would if we expected the weather to be fair); (b) the object or end toward which the expectation is directed has not been realized, at least so far as the person doing the expecting is aware; (c) the person who is expecting has grounds for believing that the end awaited is likely to occur. These conditions may not fully separate expectation from certain other processes, for example, from prediction; but they suffice to give a preliminary account of the shifts described in the epigraphs cited. Those shifts involve an alteration in each of the features enumerated. The object of expectation and thus the attitude directed toward it are finally assigned a different character from the one initially projected; the grounds for believing that what is expected will in fact occur are also revised; and the sum of these shifts is realized in the altered set of both the viewer's expectation and the realization following it.

I am concerned for the moment not so much with the consequent aspect of this experience—the jarring effect of expectation disappointed—as with what precedes it and in particular with the role of the object in initiating the process. It would be useful for conceptual economy if the relation of expecting could be represented as a transaction only between a person doing the expecting and the object or event expected, excluding other sources of information or response. That this is a plausible schematization of the cases cited is suggested by a significant omission in the accounts given by Kant and Dewey. Neither one of those accounts refers to any external factor or source of information. This is not to suppose, or to imply that Kant or Dewey suppose, that external factors do not enter into the transactions they describe. Surely, in some sense, they do. Recognition of the artificiality or naturalness of the flowers, for example, will undoubtedly employ knowledge acquired previously. But the accounts also suggest that in the last analysis the character of the expectation is founded phenomenally in the object itself—the flower or the finely wrought object—since it is there that any preconceptions which have been applied will be tested.

This point is underscored as we note that the defeat of expectation, where it occurs, is also rooted in the local source. Neither Kant nor Dewey says explicitly what information caused the shifts in attitude described by them and although the omission may be no more than inadvertent, the inadvertence itself is significant. The fact remains, so the argument here shall hold, that from whatever direction the evidence shaping expectation comes, it is finally rendered—turned into expectation and later, into its realization or defeat—on grounds provided by the object itself. Even if the evidence comes initially from a source external to the view (for example, if the person who made the artificial flowers tells us so), we judge that information finally by the object itself: we are bound to reconcile it with the object's look. The claim that the Grand Canyon is an unknown artist's earthwork, or that *The Iliad* accidentally occurred in a child's babbling, are historically irrefutable. But we respond to those objects as if we knew such claims to be false; and we do so on the basis of what we see in the objects themselves. The expectations brought to an aesthetic object often start from external indicators, for example, as we pick up a book with the title *Selected Poems* or as we view a painting titled *Normandy Landscape*. Although we may start there (and we don't necessarily do so), it is the evidence provided by the objects themselves that has the last word (the original book jacket may have been misplaced and the painting's title may reflect artistic license or irony). In effect, all the information about the work to which the viewer has access assumes a place in the view itself; it is there that the data, whatever their sources, are tested for coherence.

So far as this claim is warranted, we should be able to identify in the object the elements which determine the form of the viewer's expectation. That is, if expectations are a characteristic condition in the viewer's encounter with the work of art (and perhaps with other kinds of objects as well, but this is a separate matter); and if, as seems to be the case, such expectations are not characteristically arbitrary or whimsical, but rather tied to a particular object as expected, we then have additional reasons for believing that the variable of expectation may be formulated under another description, in terms of features discriminated in the art work rather than in the audience.

I propose that these discriminated features of the art work—the obverse side of expectation—be termed its "intentionality." [2] By that term, I refer to the *look of having an intention,* the sense afforded by the art object that *it* "intends" to realize a certain end; it is the latter which the expectation cited is expectation of, and it may be determined both in its presence and in its character by that expectation. The force of this conceptual transposition from expectation to intentionality is yet to be made clear; it is not, in all events, tied to the thesis that any context of expectation can be translated into terms of intentionality, although that may also be the case. The justification, like the thesis, is directed to the specific instance of the work of art.

It is important in this connection that the differences should be noted between "intentionality" and "intention." Intention, on most recent accounts, presupposes a conscious process of deliberation on the part of a sentient being whose intention it is. There are, in fact, reasonable conceptual grounds for hesitating to ascribe intentions to inanimate objects, notwithstanding the difficulties in winning agreement on definitions of "conscious" or "sentient." Even if inanimate objects are evocative (as are works of art), we do not ordinarily think them capable of *willing* an intentional object. To commit the Pathetic Fallacy on behalf of intentions, or even to use "intention" as a metaphor, might well obscure the distinction which the concept of intention is supposed to secure.

Intentionality, by way of contrast, imposes on the literal and substantive features of intentions an as-if quality. Assuming the pertinence of clues similar to those by which intentions are distinguished, its ascription marks the appearance of a will, apparently active in the object, without the claim of its actual presence. The aesthetic object rendered in these terms, then, is represented as giving the impression of intending an end; and this provides a key to understanding the function of that object. (It may be that the discrimination of actual intending also depends finally on this as-if factor, but it is here pertinent only to mention this possibility.) Intentionality is thus the mirror image, seen in the object itself, of the expectation pointed to by the epigraphs at the beginning of this chapter.

The specific features of intentionality in art, its extent and the reason for its power, are yet to be considered; but certain preliminary qualifications of the concept need to be entered. For one, the phenomenon of intentionality as construed here is independent of the artist's intention, either of the complex intentions which we might attribute to him personally (which could include a variety of nonartistic factors) or of what he might specifically claim to have been his intention in the creation itself. The knowledge of such intentions may contribute to a grasp of the work's intentionality; but they acquire significance in that grasp only as they are seen to converge in the work, in the work's own terms.[3] In any given case, the cues by the synthesis of which the viewer construes the work's intentionality are liable to various renderings: interpretation, we have seen, is open-ended. A grasp of those cues, furthermore, originates not only with them and the viewer: we know from other sources that symphonies do not grow, as composers do, and that lilacs blooming in the yard have not been sculpted. But the point made above about the assessment of information from sources external to the aesthetic object holds for the intentionality of art even more strongly: intentionality appears only in a present judgment of the object.

What I hope to locate through the concept of intentionality is an explanation of why the shift in context described by Kant and Dewey produces the effect they claim for it (and, by the way, a solution to the puzzle posed by Joyce). In its furthest reaches, this explanation will speak to the distinctive status of the work of art in general, as that status has been categorized in the chapters preceding this. A hint as to the nature of this explanation appears in the distinction suggested by the epigraphs between the aesthetic quality of natural objects and that of artifacts. That distinction does not imply that natural objects have no order or intentionality, but only that the order manifest in them differs characteristically from what appears in artifacts; the difference, it seems, and—if that is the case—the aesthetic effectiveness of objects generically, reflect variations in the orders and constraints which variously mark the objects. To put this preliminary argument in more standard form, there is ample evidence in the shape of objects of a close relation between form and function.

The functions of objects, natural or artificial, reflect both the manner and substance of balance, color, size (in some instances), meaning, etc. Biological functioning, it has been recognized, depends in an intricate measure on such relations;[4] and artifacts move within like constraints: differences even in artistic media, after all, impose "natural" restrictions. But to those natural limits, in the case of the objects of art, is added the complication which the artist's touch and the power of his natural sensibility provide. In some sense which we have yet to understand, it is the manner of that complication which fixes a pattern for intentionality.

The requisites for seeing through Joyce's puzzle are indicated by this still fragmentary view of the concept of intentionality. The judgment of an object and of the look it has will vary with the filtered information through which the look is discerned. It is possible that a man may rise in rage to the heights of genius—or if he were a genius, that he might create something of value even in a rage. But if either of these were pertinent factors, we could have determined this only on the basis of additional information to the single moment cited in Joyce's example. Should all such external evidence be wanting, the intentionality —the look of intention—identified in the work would be understood most responsively under the category of natural accidents: judgment on the object then would hardly differ from the response to a tree branch that had *grown* into an apparent shape. Hamlet, looking at the clouds, pointed out to Polonius what looked like a camel; in viewing a painting of a desert scene, we would not speak of seeing something that looks like a camel but of seeing a camel. That camel, obviously, cannot be ridden; but we still distinguish it from the figure which no more than looks like a camel. We make a claim for the former, then, not simply on the basis of shape or likeness alone. Other elements, for one, a knowledge of its origins, stand behind and before that look as they become part of the "look" itself.

Admittedly, such comments provide no more than indicators of the working of intentionality. They point increasingly acutely at the questions we have previously acknowledged: what it is in the work of art which constitutes intentionality, and what gives the latter—by implication, the work of art—its force. The answer to these questions, as we attribute to intentionality the appearance of a process animated by a reason, will be related to the account I have offered of reflective judgment: we see in the texture of aesthetic judgment the emergence of a reason, a shape, an order—not given in the isolated elements of an object but consequent upon them; not imposed from some external and prior context, but not independent of that context either. This "reason" has the peculiar intensity as it emerges in appearance of a performance or a doing, what has been represented here earlier as the adhesion manifested in aesthetic proximity. The translation among these concepts remains to be made more precisely and in further detail.

The Terms of Intentionality. If intentionality located in the art work is the mirror image of expectation as reported of the viewer, then the conditions of expectation should be evident (in their obverse sides) as conditions of intentionality. The three conditions cited can be compressed as two in this new appearance: (a) that the elements in the work of art which define its intentionality acquire coherence as another element is "discerned" which is not itself one of them; (b) that together these elements indicate or point to in the object an end or goal to be realized and also the means by which it is to be realized.

The logical status and the relation of these conditions will be examined later. That analysis would be irrelevant, however, if intentionality were not acknowledged as phenomenon. The key point in this connection is the emphasis on intentionality as an appearance; for while this feature is in some ways a liability, it also suggests that certain requirements we might otherwise impose are precluded. The as-if character of intentionality, I have suggested, not only *reveals* itself in appearance, but is in its nature an appearance. Unlike the determination of intentions which requires evidence attesting that a look is grounded in fact as well as in appearance, the identification of intentionality is no more than a discrimination of appearance. The key to the discernment of intentions is the "finding of a reason in a process";[5] for intentionality, where the question is left open as to whether such reasons are in fact reasons, the examiner must be satisfied with the *look* of a "reason in a process." The two phenomena may be alike so far as regards the impossibility of determining their presence independently of appearances; the significant difference between them turns on what we claim to be able to extract from those appearances.

The questions on which I focus beyond this point have in common the purpose of distinguishing aesthetic intention (intentionality) from other kinds of intention. It has been admitted, for one thing, that the quality of intentionality may not be peculiar to the aesthetic moment: non or less aesthetic processes may also answer to the conditions stated which conclude in the look of an intention. It may even be, I have suggested, that the conditions for the identification of intentions include the discrimination of intentionality. If intentionality is to be a distinctive feature of the aesthetic moment, then, we should be able to identify the specific aspect of intentionality which distinguishes that moment. Second, and whatever the resolution of this first issue is, the question remains of how intentionality becomes a feature of the moments in which it appears and of the aesthetic moment in particular: what structural conditions does it presuppose, and what does it imply for the experience in which it is rendered?

Consider, as a means of approaching the former of these questions, the issue of how we determine the presence of intentions. In the attribution of intentions, although what the agent of an action says about his intention is relevant to the conclusions drawn, his words (if there are any) are hardly regarded as decisive. We measure the words about what he intended by a more inclusive criterion, specifically what he does, his words being part of this. Perhaps, as Kant suggested in his account of the Good Will, we cannot ever be certain of anyone's intentions, even our own; it is clear at any rate that when we have exhausted the evidence of agency, there is no place else to turn: intentions have no visible form in themselves. Thus, the identification of intentions runs parallel initially to that of intentionality. Although in judgments of moral actions, we attribute the intention embodied in the actions to a person rather than to an object, we do so on grounds similar to those which figure in aesthetic judgment: namely, what happens in the process. The difficulty of deciding for a work of art what its intentionality is continues the parallel between that process and the identification of intentions. This difficulty has been clearly exemplified in the receptions accorded new art forms. A recurrent feature of "revolutions" in art is the bewilderment of the audience not only at what the new forms do, but at what they even hope to accomplish, what they are attempting. Difficulties in grasping a particular work might arise, of course, even if the viewer knew what was being attempted. But at many notable transitions in the history of the arts, this lack of comprehension has reflected a lack of understanding of the ends sought by the new art forms, forms which may eventually turn out to be so unexceptionable as Balzac's naturalism or the use of light in Impressionist painting.

Other, more restricted instances of the same kind of difficulty may make the point more sharply. An audience which hears a joke that is not funny will usually recognize from the structure of which the joke was part that what was intended was indeed a joke. Again: the audience sees a character undergoing misfortune after misfortune, and finds the intended tragic stature to be lacking. But before the audience can reach either of these conclusions, they must have ruled out the possibilities that what had been intended was a bad joke or that it was not a joke that had been intended at all but the parody of a joke; or, in the other example, that the unheroic heroine had been presented in the development of a theme that heroic stature is not possible in a particular stage of society. Such decisions, although they reflect a characteristic procedural difficulty in determining intentionality, argue still more basically for the *possibility* of that determination; such decisions are made and are necessary.

In these examples, the differences between intentionality and intention assert themselves clearly. For one, intentions are ascribed to agents, not to actions. The agent, moreover, must meet certain conditions that are independent of any particular action for which he is responsible. He must, for example, be capable of foreseeing the consequences of certain actions (one can hardly intend to do something while acting either indifferently or to avoid doing it). That capacity, by definition, must be persistent, not restricted to a single act. Intentionality, in contrast, does not presuppose an agent; in the absence of contrary evidence, it can appear in objects which are the result of no intentions at all (witness, again, Dewey's example). Even to know that an instance of intentionality is the consequence of certain intentions is not necessarily to acknowledge the conditions set by the latter on the former. One may read an artist's plans for a work which was never executed, understanding from them that he had intentions of a certain scope or magnitude. But those intentions are different, in some cases very different, from what we have spoken of as the work's intentionality—what appears in the completed artifact—to which the only access, finally, is by way of the work itself. Often enough we find that the artist's words on his work are irrelevant or misleading; Raphael without arms might still have been a genius—but it is obvious that we would then have had no access to what we *now* know of his genius.

The distinction thus marked between intentionality and intention may seem invidious insofar as it compares two dissimilar settings, the one focused on an object, the other involving an object and its source. Perhaps if the comparison were made between works of art and other objects, the proposed distinctiveness of aesthetic intentionality would lose its force. Consider, for example, a scientific theory, for the moment regarded as an object. One might argue that in it, too, we can read off intentionality as it answers the conditions cited. Yet significant differences persist. For the designation of intentionality in the theory—its own form—unavoidably lapses into the consideration of intentions. The elements constituting the theory and thus its appearance, aspects which in the work of art fully define its intentionality, explicitly point in the theory to an external purpose or intention: the solving of a problem. We expect, even require, a theory to respond to questions that circulate independently of the theory itself, concerning patterns of human behavior or planetary motion or geometric relations. That expectation is not arbitrary or beside the point of the theory: the latter is inexplicable aside from such conditions. (This is not to say, of course, that a theory may not be viewed aesthetically; but the latter aesthetic occurrence would presuppose the structure of the theory as described.)

The shape of the aesthetic intention is not set prior to the aesthetic moment, either in a human source or in a projected end. This fact has been reflected in the unsuccessful attempts to give an account of art on the grounds of external intention, for example, in those which refer the substance of art to its psychological origins. It may be that something more will yet be achieved by such efforts; judged by their accomplishments, however, they only obscure the principal issue affecting the aesthetic moment, specifically, the aesthetic character of art. Such analyses of great works of art or great artists—for example, Freud's works on Leonardo and Dostoyevsky—reach conclusions which are substantively no different from those conclusions reached in the analysis of paintings by children or psychotics. We learn something from those accounts about the psychological state of the artist as human being, but little about the features which mark a great work of art or about the work of art as art.

An additional source of support for the distinction is the capacity of intentionality for innovation and variety. It is true that human intentions also vary and are open to evolution; but their variety has been limited, and those limits have not been gratuitous. Patterns appear not only among individual intentions, but in the forms in which they accumulate—in political institutions, for example, and economic systems. Such consistent patterns, reflecting the constancy of the problems to which they respond, are, however, absent from the forms of art. The limitations which control the origins of intended actions also constrain the ends which they realize: both are governed by practical functions and are limited by the range of primary practical needs. Art and the forms of aesthetic vision, on the other hand, although limited by specific media and by the artist's capacity for working them, have fewer constraints; the question even of what are to be media is as open, indefinitely if not infinitely, as is the capacity of the artist to enlarge on them.

This is not to deny that cycles or patterns can be identified within the art of individual cultures and periods; but the diversity of style and form evident in the arts markedly distinguishes objects of art from other accomplishments of culture. Precisely because they do not come as answers to predetermined or external problems, they embody a larger measure of diversity and freedom. The work of art, as distinct from intended actions with their imposition of a will on an object, presupposes independence or openness in the medium. The media of art set characteristic boundaries; but such boundaries, even at their most extreme, are less stringent than they would be under the constraints of external intentions. This aspect of the distinction between intention and intentionality is sharply focused in the difference between the arts and the crafts. The craft of cabinet making, for example, reflects a prior intention as painting does not: whatever else a cabinet may do or be, it must provide a storage space for objects. (And objects, furthermore, are likely to need to be stored.) This does not mean that a cabinet may not be an aesthetic object, but that its possibilities of aesthetic articulation are fixed by a dominant and restrictive practical consideration. If it sounds invidious to distinguish in this way between cabinets and paintings, the common divisions of the arts (as, for example, between arts and crafts or between the major and minor arts) points unequivocally in that direction.

Based as the relation between intention and intentionality is on the *appearance* of the distinction, a further reflection on the distinction may take shape as an objection. In moral appreciation or judgment, reference to intention is, if not a sufficient condition, at least a necessary one. But it might be argued that there is no like requirement for intentionality in aesthetic appreciation: the fact that the concept has not often been mentioned in accounts of aesthetic value might itself be regarded as testimony against its pertinence. If anything (so the objection), more emphasis has been placed on the concept of intention even with respect to aesthetic value than on intentionality. We may acknowledge, for example, that the artist works from something on the order of an intention, if only in the abstract sense that he is in the end responsible for the production of an object of a particular kind of interest. Admittedly, this is to say little more than that, however the artist produces his work, he is unlikely to do so by accident. Formally, furthermore, this acknowledgment pertains not only to works of art but to any artifacts or actions whatsoever; it recognizes only that the process leading up to the object is indeed a process and not a mere series of events. Moreover, the analogous justification for speaking of intentionality in art might be contested. It could be argued, in fact, that the latter concept only introduces a redundancy into the already complex critical process. The joke that falls flat, the tragic or not-so-tragic heroine, the development of a musical theme: each may be just that. Why speak in addition, multiplying the entities, about the appearance-of-an-intention which is or is not realized?

The claim of the lack of historical references to intentionality would not, in any event, be decisive in assessing the use of that concept; but it is worth noting that in certain important analyses of aesthetic judgment, preeminently in Kant's, the concept of intentionality has figured largely. I might add, furthermore, that instances of ordinary linguistic usage support the distinction proposed. A common expression of adverse criticism among contemporary painters, for example, is that a painting "doesn't work." It may not always be explicit, even to him, what the viewer who says this thinks would work, but the logical conditions of the expression are evident: that an attempt to accomplish a particular purpose within the frame of the object has failed; and that this, both the attempt and the failure, are visible in the object itself. A similar logical basis seems to hold as well for such common critical judgments as that the "object does/does not achieve what it set out to."

The need to take account of such responses to art would be substantial quite aside from the contention which I infer from them, that they are a symptom of a fundamental characteristic of art. The claim here, yet to be substantiated, is both that intentionality figures in the appreciation of art, and that it is pertinent to the effort of understanding that process—thus, by implication, to a grasp of the process of art itself.

More needs to be said about the way intentionality is fulfilled or not in the object. Even at this point, however, a connection will be evident between intentionality and the structure of reflective judgment which has been the key concept in the analysis leading up to it. The conditions of intentionality approximate closely those which have defined reflective judgment and its denotative component. Reflective judgment, again, is not given in the syntactic elements of the work, nor is it composed simply of elements drawn from the work's exterior. It affords a means whereby the elements of the work, otherwise isolated and fragmented, are seen to be articulated and to achieve coherence. The justifications for the parallel sets of conditions governing the two concepts are also similar. Imagine, with respect to the first condition cited for intentionality, the attempt to view a work of art under the stipulation that one was restricted in that view to the apparent least elements of the work, for example, to the dictionary meanings of individual words, and had no access to an overarching principle that comprehended those elements. Imagine again, with respect to the second condition, an aesthetically relevant object on which such a principle *had* been imposed, but which was either independent of any direction obtained from the given work, or with respect to which the individual elements of the work offered no cumulative support. In the former of these cases, the art work would be experienced as an unrelated series of happenings; in the latter, the art work itself would be left untouched by the principle imposed. There would emerge, quite simply, two disjointed entities or groups of elements, neither of which provided a hint of the coherence or pointed articulation which we characteristically find in the aesthetic moment. It is no mere metaphor to speak of the art work as trying or attempting to accomplish a certain end: we find in enough, and especially in enough significant, art works that an end is reached which would be quite inexplicable except in terms of a design, to warrant the location of an intention internal to the object itself.

Again, the identification of intentionality in any given case may be contestable. The "true believer" who thinks it consonant with reason to see the world in terms of God the Creator or of some other supervening consciousness will undoubtedly find the evidence of intentionality as well as that of intentions in all of the processes and qualities of that world. The consistent skeptic (if he is possible at all), trusting only to the rigor of his own skepticism, will find no process anywhere else and thus probably not even the semblance of order required for intentionality: thus the influence of predisposition on vision. It is less important for the moment to resolve such possibilities of discrepancy, however, than to note that in them, too, the phenomenon of intentionality can be meaningfully disputed. The fact that vision may encounter unclarity or ambiguity in some of its efforts is balanced by its accomplishments in others, the test of judgment in every case being whether the elements of the work could make the sense which the viewer makes of them without the contrivance of a structure or order of the sort indicated. That the application of this criterion may sometimes be cumbersome—one point of Joyce's example—is less significant than the fact that its applicability is sometimes evident: the principal point of Joyce's example and of the others as well. Finally, of course, the justification for adducing the concept of intentionality in connection with the work of art will be evident (or not) in the appearance of the work itself.

The Logic of Intentionality. The characterization given of intentionality requires elaboration if only because its ramifications—both of the concept and of the phenomenon—spread widely. Not so much as a virtue as a matter of necessity, what is finally involved in the scrutiny of the objects or processes which provide a ground for intentionality are aspects of the structure of any object or process whatsoever. To locate the conditions of intentionality is to have traced them to contexts where it does not appear or where its appearance is not so marked, as well as to those other contexts in which it is prominent. Thus, in effect, to *all* the intelligible contexts to which we have access.

The evidence from which the present attempt sets out is the prima facie fact of intentionality. That fact at the very least reflects an ordering of elements in the work, a relational pattern. The functioning of such a pattern is evident both in the examples cited originally in this chapter and in the conditions for intentionality derived from those examples; it is presupposed in the related claim, disclosed by the analysis, that intentionality in the aesthetic object characteristically culminates in an order of realization. For even if the realization which intentionality invites is blocked, this failure becomes comprehensible through the juxtaposition within the larger whole of two orders—one, of the initial impulse; the other, of its realization, of which even frustration would be a variety. This attribution of order presupposes no specific medium or occasion; as designated so far, any material or occasion may serve. Such tolerance requires a corresponding breadth in the parameters of order. This requirement can be met, I propose, by construing the order in terms of a serial or presentational parameter, an aspect of the members of which points to a related aspect in every other one of the members.[6]

By a presentational order I mean a non-random progression to which the elements provide a specific character by their relations to each other. Consider the form of presentational structure in its simplest appearances. The clearest example of such an order will be found in a series of elements bound by a single factor (for reasons to be mentioned such a neatly restricted order is unlikely to occur in fact). This would be the case in a structure of the following sequence: *i, ii, iii, iiii, iiiii, iiiiii, iiiiiii* . . . in which the specific factor apparently is the addition of an *i*. I say "apparently" because additional factors may emerge as the sequence progresses and because this factor may itself be reducible to others. If we assume this to be the single distinguishing factor of the sequence cited, however, the grounds of the claim made previously concerning the relations among the elements of such an order become evident. Two points are notable in the analysis of any one of the elements of this sequence; first, that the factor taken to be an essential feature of all the individual elements, comes to light only as the individual elements are juxtaposed to the others in the sequence. The factor is thus a function of the parts of the order. Secondly, as that articulation is discerned, the overarching order or form of the entire sequence also emerges; one sees where the sequence will end and, for any stopping point in that sequence, what the whole amounts to. This claim is underscored by the contrast produced if we introduced *i* again as the next member of the series, after *iiiiiii*. If the series includes no more than this single addition, we will undoubtedly be more puzzled than we had been as to what the series as a whole amounts to—what, in effect, the series is—not because there are no possible explanations which could be given of this new addition, but because the context is now more indefinite than it had been. As initially proposed, the elements present an order in terms of which each element and the whole which they together comprise makes sense—an order which is unsettled and is thrown (again) into question with the addition of the *i* at the end of the sequence.

In more complicated and more common patterns of expression, it will be proportionately difficult to identify the factors which link the elements of an order and correspondingly difficult to identify the order of the whole. As a consequence of these difficulties, the task of determining the extent to which the presentational order is realized or frustrated also becomes harder; and such difficulties were amply attested in chapter 3, in the attempt there to identify the factors underlying the denotative force of the nonliterary arts. My contention is not that such obstacles can be ignored, however, but that finally, so far as the entities in connection with which they appear matter aesthetically, they yield. The presentational order of intentionality depends on a linkage of the elements within that order. That linkage in fact comprises the order; and it is as we see the order emerge, with all the varieties of tone and meaning which serve as linkage, that the aesthetic object makes its appearance. That order is one of the things, at least, that the object amounts to.

This claim suggests that intentionality will be a feature of all objects or events. It is not my purpose, however, to pursue so broad a thesis, but rather to show how, given it, the distinctive features ascribed to the aesthetic object can be accounted for. The argument is focused, then, on the factors which operate in the intentionality of art. To be sure, these cannot be disclosed, in the absence of a particular object, for that object or for its kind. But the formal character of a genre of experience may nonetheless be distinguishable—in this case, what would appear as the aesthetic factor. That factor has been indicated in the analysis of the Modes of Articulation in the preceding chapter. On the basis of the distinction drawn among the various modes, I suggested that the aesthetic moment represented a convergence of the modes of Denotation and Sequence. Those modes characterized the aesthetic moment in terms, with respect to the former mode, of Translucence, and, with respect to the latter, of Persistence. With the convergence of those modes, the aesthetic moment denoted not a free theoretical object, but joined the drive toward such an object to another one which turned the viewer back to the appearance of the initial object. The denotation of the aesthetic object, then, both extends beyond the object itself and to a projection initially and continuously asserted there. The role of Persistence marks off in this process a quality of passage which strikes a balance between the internalization and the externalization of history, opposed to either the simple passage of discrete instants or to atemporal dislocation. The aesthetic factor thus denotes both *in* and *beyond* the object, marking the temporal transition or hinge between a given generality and a particular future yet to be contrived.

If we translate this account into the idiom of intentionality, we see in its rendering of the aesthetic object features which are independently recognizable. Where in any instance of intentionality, attention is drawn to the elements in the order of articulation and, separately, to the overarching order of purpose, in the work of art, those two aspects of intentionality explicitly converge. Each contrives and reinforces the other. The intention or will of the aesthetic object pushes forward; but even as that intention is articulated, the resultant order reflects backward on the elements producing it. These two vectors set up a dynamic in which the work gives the appearance of attempting to realize an end, of going beyond the elements to an object intended, and of being turned back in that attempt toward the elements the articulation of which provides the initial impetus. The work of art, in other terms, both represents (beyond itself) and presents (itself)—each of those processes linked to the other.

The question may be raised as to the relation between intentionality, on the one hand, and its realization or lack of it, on the other; the latter seems summarily to have become an aspect of intentionality itself, although the conditions cited for intentionality made no reference to it. But an answer to this question is indicated in what has been said about the process of which intentionality is a central feature. In that process an elliptical order emerges: its impulse is to move beyond the elements comprising it, but it is constantly driven back to them. As this occurs, the shape of intentionality itself is duplicated; that is, the elements form themselves again, but this time against the background now provided by the first level of intentionality. This process of duplication may itself be duplicated, but the essential contrast is set in the first delineation of impulse and response. This does not mean that the presentational order, as a consequence of the contrast, is complete as the contrast is first recognizable. The elements which make up the order are, as we saw in chapters 2 and 3, not the isolated syntactic elements which one might identify at first glance in the aesthetic object, but reflective elements of denotation which even if they are formally "given" in the object, by implication expand beyond it as well. The features of intentionality cited are not peculiar to the aesthetic moment; they are prominent there because of their distinctive convergence and the conceptual net which they cast over what might otherwise seem such unrelated phenomena as reflective judgment, denotation, and aesthetic proximity. So far as this is the case, the charge that intentionality is conceptually redundant—that to speak of what the art work accomplishes would be sufficient without positing an attempt on its part to be something—although perhaps pertinent for any single aesthetic moment, loses its force. Even for those moments where intentionality and realization coincide, where, caught up by art itself, one might be content to ignore the conceptual issues in favor of the aesthetic object, still the concept of intentionality contributes understanding. And it could do so only insofar as it mirrored the aesthetic process.

The question that initiates reflective judgment is, in the formulation given earlier, "What does the work amount to?" That question presupposes in its answer reference to all the elements of the work (however they be identified). This identification is now referred to as the phenomenon of intentionality, principally because it makes sense or a whole of the several leading concepts in terms of which the work of art has been described in this analysis. Intentionality, it might be claimed, lays the ground for reflective judgment as a phenomenon. In its specific appearances, intentionality defines the form which perception and understanding of the particular work follow—so far as the work succeeds or fails. By it the aesthetic moment is ascribed a tendency toward coherence, as if the moment itself were willing that coherence. Only as we do this, and are willing to speak openly of the work's intention (or at least take it for granted), can we give full value to the coherence and significance which art in fact offers.

What has been said about intentionality and the presentational order may suggest that what finally has emerged here is a variation on formalist accounts of art. Superficially, intentionality and the orders which sponsor it seem to be internal items of the work of art; it is apparently not the texture or media or meanings of the aesthetic object which shape intentionality, but rather the formal relations among the elements which would then act as isolated and pure sensation. But this resurrection of the distinction between sensation and reference could be sustained only if the elements entering the form of intentionality were confined in their import to their linear significance. It has been shown in the terms so far presented that this need not be the case; on other terms, principally what we know of the aesthetic moment itself, it is quite evidently not the case. The factors qualifying articulation in the art work may produce a significant presentational order, and will, in fact, be more likely to do this—given the impulse for articulation in both the artist and his audience—than to produce an order which is merely formal. This probability is reinforced by the fact that order of itself may be significant, and not only formally significant, for man.

In the common appearances of aesthetic order, it is quite clear that such order is not itself linear or flat. Media vary, to be sure, in the type of impress which they can "take"; but they share at least the capacity for being impressed. (The latter phrase might serve as a definition of what a medium is.) The tension between representation and presentation ascribed to intentionality is not exclusively or perhaps even principally formal in dimension. We may well say (approvingly) for a particular art work, that its intentions are realized; it has accomplished what it set out to do. But this in turn raises the question of what the significance is of what the work set out to do. And *that* question, it seems evident, does not move the analysis beyond the aesthetic context, in search of an extra-aesthetic explanation, but asks rather for a more sustained analysis of the same features which initially suggested the aesthetic presence. The question which formalist theories of art have consistently failed to answer is the question of what is significant about art's form; the fact that formalists might try to speak of Significant Form did not, as the work of Clive Bell and Roger Fry demonstrates, blunt the point of that question. Form, on the terms of the formalist, is usually a visual metaphor restricted to the occurrence of line or configuration; but it is only as meaning or denotation are also acknowledged as possessors or sponsors of form and thus of the aesthetic presence, that formalist accounts can hope to be adequate.

The individual appearances of art do not take shape as purely sensuous transactions. The forms of art stretch over various bodies which make a difference not only to the appearance but to the import of the forms themselves. This fact is reflected, for example, in the differences between natural and artistic sources of the aesthetic moment. Certain aspects of those two sources, it seems clear, are shared; either of them, in any event, may be relevant aesthetically. This claim is not simply a reassertion of the aesthetic potentiality of any object whatever; it represents an empirical thesis that certain objects or situations deriving from either source have special aesthetic power both as compared to other members of the same classes and as compared to some members of the other class. That power can be construed in terms of the form of intentionality and the ordering which it represents. The traditional category of the sublime in nature may require distinctive grounds, although even it functions by *transcending* patterns of order; in natural forms on a lesser scale, for example, a countryside landscape or a flower, the patterns of intentionality are more immediately apparent. A persistent characteristic of such natural forms is their simplicity, a lack of tension between expectation and fulfillment which is as much a measure of the lack of complexity of those aspects as it is of the way they are fitted to each other in appearance. To describe this ready conformity as a distinctive and inviting aesthetic feature, moreover, is not as ad hoc as it might sound. We recognize natural beauty in fact; and we also recognize, by its side, the contrasting and larger emphasis on artistic form in contrast to that of nature. To be sure, there are museums of natural beauty (parks, preserves, zoos). Yet it seems clear that the greater measure of what have been cited here as features of the aesthetic moment pertain to artifacts rather than to natural sources—a conclusion which is reinforced by the attribution to the aesthetic moment generically of an hierarchy of order. Artifacts share as a class, and thus as a factor in their order, a maker who contributes to their structure various shapes of his design. This factor adds to the natural material of a medium the possibility of forms or patterns of articulation which, left to itself, the medium would unavoidably lack. This is, I take it, at least in part what Croce means in writing that "Next to art, nature is dumb." Not that nature does not speak—but that the limitations on what it can say impede it in comparison to the vocabulary of artifacts.

The Lure of the Aesthetic. Even if we accept the reconstruction of the aesthetic moment in terms of intentionality, the question as to how that moment exerts its power, of what the lure of the aesthetic is, remains untouched. The convergence of intentionality and realization might be a useful conceptual means of characterizing the objects of art, but by itself that characterization does little to explain the impact of art on its viewers or to answer the question of why art should have come into existence in the first place. This omission in the foregoing account has not been gratuitous: I have been searching for a conceptual framework by which, as a foundation for explanation, the phenomenon might first be identified. But those two projects, although formally distinguishable, converge in fact. So far as categories of identification or classification pertain to a subject matter, they foreshadow, albeit tendentiously, the grounds of its appearance as well as the appearance itself. Left at that level, however, the foreshadowing is incomplete; it narrows the alternatives open to explanation without committing itself. And this in turn places a large burden on the movement of explanation: if the evidence is exhausted (as it should be) in locating the phenomenon, in relating and distinguishing it, what more can be called on by the explanation which reaches beyond it? There is, it would seem, nothing left over which explanation could add.

Thus, the question which finally emerges at the end of our discussion—Why the lure of art?—bears watching on methodological grounds. Any answer given will probably turn out to be if not simply ad hoc, a variation on such explanation. An example can be cited which, as it caricatures the problem, makes the point sharply. It would be an explanation of sorts to say that interest in games and sports, which apparently crosses all cultural and historical boundaries of human society, is due to a specific impulse in man—that "man by nature is a games-loving animal." But this account, by itself, is not very illuminating. It contributes little to an understanding either of human nature or of the interest in games in particular; it seems to reiterate the initial assertion of the phenomenon, adding only the illusion of a causal explanation to it. (This objection is the usual and overworked point of the behavioristic criticism of appeals in biology and psychology to the concept of instinct.) It might be argued, in fact, that the appeal to a concept of human nature for an explanation of a type of activity is *necessarily* redundant, that as a concept of human nature is derived or inferred, it will at best be no more than a repetition of the items of evidence; at its worst, it selects from that evidence to provide a simplified, and tendentious, account.

It should be noted, however, that this objection, if it holds at all, holds not only for putative explanations of human nature, but indeed for any explanation whatever: we could hardly deny that an explanation which fails to reach beyond the evidence initially presented, in the terms provided by that evidence, would not explain very much at all. Thus, unless we wish to rule out either the use of explanation in general or the appeal to human nature as a particular instance of explanation, the objections to such formulations as man's "games-loving" nature must have different grounds.

One obvious objection to the appeal to man's sportive nature is that not only is it directed to a single set of man's activities, but that it leaves untouched and without argument the variety of other activities which engage him: it does not have the covering power required of such an explanation. This does not mean that any such statement must, to be acceptable, comprehend all of these activities, but that if it does not do this, it may yet be expected to locate itself with respect to the appearances of human action to which it does not apply. The most significant accounts which have been given of human nature—as broad as the differences otherwise are between Aristotle and Freud, Plato and Marx—are marked by their common illumination of a variety of evidence concerning human activity and experience. Aristotle's assertion at the beginning of the *Metaphysics*, for example, that all men by nature desire to know, is intended as a response both to evidence cited in the immediate context concerning man the theoretician and to analyses in other contexts, for instance, in the account of *mimesis* and man's enjoyment of tragedy in the *Poetics*. Such comprehensiveness is a crucial element in the force of Aristotle's thesis, whether it be finally persuasive or not. It seems clear, independently of this example, that if distinct impulses or appeals to nature were posited for each aspect or moment of man's activities, they could not serve as explanations at all.

In our attempt to understand the lure of art, we shall then have to say something more than that man by nature is drawn to the creation or appreciation of art; at least we must show, if we say only that, that this supposed impulse is substantively prior to a number of others. And some such account should emerge (this would be a test on all sides) as we relate the presentational order defined in the concept of intentionality to the concept of reflective judgment and to the latter's attendant notions of denotation and aesthetic proximity. These concepts, pointed singly and together toward the phenomenon of art and the discourse about it, would be pertinent only insofar as they successfully embodied a distinction between certain moments and other moments for which they had no or less relevance. They conclude in an effort to place the aesthetic moment in a larger context, and this sense of comprehension should, if it is to be effective, carry through to an account of the lure of art.

The formal conditions required of such an explanation are less easily defined. I have spoken in chapter 1 of the features of philosophical explanation in general and the kinds of problems involved in their formulation. The two criteria of adequacy cited in that discussion were the principles of Coherence and Applicability, and supervening on them, the sense finally that explanations should indeed explain. The objections to which these criteria are liable have been indicated; my intention in the present context is not to argue that issue further, but to see how they are met.

The direction to be taken by the last stage of this account, on the two sides of art and of its audience, has already been intimated. The relation between the intentionality of art and reflective judgment joins the means by which the body of art evokes a response. Intentionality, I have suggested, affords a form for reflective judgment, the form "in" the object which the aesthetic judgment, with its process of performance and its assertion of a distinctive variety of denotation, articulates. In the convergence of these aspects of the aesthetic moment—from the objective pole of intentionality and the subjective pole of reflective judgment—three components can be identified which then define that moment: (a) the presentational order—that is, an order in which a place is assigned to each of the elements of the order, each of them reflecting and qualifying the force of each of the other elements; (b) indeterminacy—that is, a characteristic openness in the discrimination of the order, an openness which although it follows the direction of the response, finally bases that response on the discrimination of the moment itself as the latter involves the active presence of the viewer; (c) projection—that is, the emergence of a relation between the presentational order and the indeterminacy in its discrimination, which consummates the moment as a unified whole in the field of vision of the viewer and finally in the viewer himself. These components, it will be noted, are not temporally separated; to conceive of any one of them independently of the others is to lose both the substance and the formal structure of the whole. Each of them has been previously defined, the notion of presentational order earlier in this chapter, the two other components in earlier chapters. The description of indeterminacy and projection appeared first in the terms of reflective judgment, in the claim that the substance of the judgment is not simply given in the elements of the object of aesthetic experience, but is performed or projected there. There is neither a past nor a future fact from which that present can be deduced. The judgment is open not because the objects of aesthetic attentiveness happen to be opaque, but because in their nature they afford the viewer, whatever their internal resolutions or denouements, an opening in experience, a sense of the live possibility which he himself may yet realize. The project realized is the judgment and the self which emerges as a function of that judgment.[7]

To call for the derivation or "justification" of these components is in effect to call for a Transcendental Deduction: a ground that both reveals them as explanatory and which establishes itself as necessary. I have referred in the Introduction to the problematic status of such deductions, although that disclaimer as a general principle need not be argued here. Still, the need which the deduction would fill persists, if the components outlined (and thus the project which they complete) are to have a point. I suggest a variation on that project which at once avoids the claim of necessity and yet renders an account; as a thesis, it is portentous—but its claim needs to be stated boldly. It holds that the components of the aesthetic moment cited converge as a condition of selfhood, of the existence of the self as its form and activities are manifest. They may not be the only components pertinent to such an account, nor are they a priori necessary (thus the major break with the criteria for a Transcendental Deduction). They serve as conditions which, given the self as we find it, explicate it. Put slightly differently, the self is possible so far as those conditions obtain.

The demonstration of this encompassing thesis calls not for proof that the phenomenon of art is possible, but for an explanation of that possibility, unavoidably returning the analysis to the self for whom the aesthetic phenomenon appears. In one sense, such claims for the integral importance of the elements discriminated to the existence of the self would require consideration of all the appearances and evidence that pertain to the self. The danger in avoiding such an undertaking is that the thesis offered may turn out to be as empty as it is large, reducing to the commonplace claim, for example, that after all, man is a symbol-making animal. To be sure, something of that commonplace is asserted here. But to it is appended the claim that whatever other elements this symbol-making impulse embodies, it includes preeminently a predisposition to the aesthetic moment. The claim is thus offered that the aesthetic moment is a paradigm among the various moments which shape experience— that any other or less-aesthetic moments can be, in effect will have to be, comprehended in its terms. The fact is (this at least can be demonstrated) that the components of the aesthetic moment cited—presentational order, indeterminacy, projection —are categories which apply widely, to components of experience for which we would not initially or predominantly assign the term "aesthetic." They adhere, I would argue, even if in any particular case they do not end as art does, to the form and substance of all activity—to dialing a telephone, to making an ethical decision, to gossiping about the neighbors. A more basic claim underwriting this one, then, is that other moments could not be accounted for without the asthetic moment. It shapes them not only in their forms, but in the very possibility that they should have those forms at all; the self, determined in the aesthetic moment, is a condition for them too.

The "deduction" of this thesis is at once present and prospective. It is prospective in the sense that it is a function of and may thus be altered by evidence other than that cited here; it is also, more fundamentally, a function of possible changes in the self on which it presumes—changes which might, for example, render the world of art obsolete or defunct. But the deduction is most basically present as a formulation of the conditions for *any* judgment or experience—given the varieties of judgment and experience which we recognize. All human judgment or action presupposes a presentational order, in the judgment or action if not in its object; that presentational order is itself open to the same contrivance and openness in consciousness which produced it: thus, a ground for the general condition of indeterminacy. And finally, those two conditions *necessarily* yield the possibility of their synthesis—consciousness molding the presentational order—which from the viewpoint of the subject in this process, I have spoken of as the act of "projection."

These conditions preeminently characterize the basis of the aesthetic moment; we have seen quite distinctly their appearances, singly and together, in that context. But the recognition of them in that moment reverberates in the other instances of judgment which have been cited. Thus, the referral of the lure of art to the conditions of the self would be something more than simply an ad hoc appeal for the significance of art even if it were to turn out to be in some respects inadequate or mistaken.

The articulation of elements thus ascribed to the aesthetic

moment is not the evolutionary, organic emergence which Dewey ascribes to the "consummatory" experience, although the two accounts are similar in other aspects. In Dewey also the elements which run through experience of art are interrelated, in some sense, cotemporal, none having significance without the others; nor do they lead to a condition of stasis: they serve, not necessarily but in fact, a larger and longer process. But the differences are no less marked. Where for Dewey the consummatory experience is defined internally, of materials one assumes to be already present or given,[8] in the pattern described here the materials, what is imposed on them and the end reached share an intrinsic feature of indeterminacy—if not quite *ex nihilo,* certainly from mere potentiality—which is refined as the whole emerges. Man, the artist or viewer, is not simply and one-sidedly the maker: he is himself made in the aesthetic moment, clarified and projected further than he had been or known. The process affords him a representative, an image which is important to him because it is only through such representatives that he asserts himself as a self and not as a stone or a flower or an idea in God's mind.

As the intentionality of the work of art unfolds, it involves the observer in its process. The intentionality is not something that simply appears or happens to him; its form, and the form of its realization, end by becoming his form. The empathy theorists may have overstated their case as they thought to attach man to certain particular physical movements of the art work; but their intuition of the eidetic impression of art is a profound metaphor. What I have referred to as the denotation of art is not a reference made to an independent structure, shaped and completed by itself, which the observer addresses as himself complete and detached. The work does not engage beliefs about isolated aspects of an external world; it strikes at the center of the viewer's engagements—which, after all, begin and end with the articulation of the self which is emergent in the process. That this takes place especially in response to the aesthetic moment implies a corresponding impulse that moves him to it. A spider would weave a web around art's objects as readily as around any others; it is little enough to claim that the distinctiveness in man's response to art originates, at one of its sources, in him.

Seen as a reconstruction of process or history, the same account will require only a slightly different form. Like all finite entities, man is *in* history, an object on which events and other objects act and leave their mark; in this regard he does not differ from other entities in the world—in the range from stones to ideas. In addition to this background in history, however, man is also *of* history, in a manner foreign to those others. The recognition that this is so is itself an indelible and constant feature of his experience. Indeed it might be argued that there is no more fundamental source from which he draws than that recognition—the "I" thinking and knowing the "I"; no one which so persistently animates or recurs in the categories of human experience. The sense of presentational order as indeterminate and projective, its manifestation in the expectation and retrospection of particular events, in the identification of the self with respect to any event and of itself as individual, amounts in the process to a constitution of experience as such.

The formal structure ascribed to intentionality has been seen to encompass a recognizable purpose forward and the realization to which it reaches. The character of that process is disclosed formally in the concept of presentational order. This same concept, in the distinctive variation it ascribes to the aesthetic moment, defines the peculiar power of the aesthetic moment. In its broadest outline, the affinity for it presupposes an impulse for what might be referred to as reduplication: a charter or ground of experience in man which looks for representation in the orders of his expression and, in particular, in the order of art. This impulse for exemplification and expansion may reveal itself in a number of forms; indeed, on the argument given here, it is a feature of all the manners of human expression. But the work of art is paradigmatic among these manners in that it not only reveals this impulse, but reveals it as a *characteristic* feature of man: the process, open yet not arbitrary, which is a condition first of aesthetic experience and then of human experience as such.

That impulse is not toward mere knowledge, the cognition in abstract form of what lies on the far side of immediate presence, as if what lay beyond was already and simply there, but of *being* beyond them, with the grasp this gives man not only of his past and his future, but of the present in which they and he meet.[9] It is not that process is banished in or by art. It is that by way of art man in effect *becomes* process, or presentational order—which is what in process matters most for him: drawing the random or attenuated elements of an object and of the experience in which it is an element to a point. He accomplishes this formally, as maker and viewer, by reconstructing in intentionality the shape of process; he accomplishes this materially by finding himself in the appearances which form takes, as those appearances summon the powers of projection and assertion and the impulse to exercise those powers on the part of art's audience.

There is in this account—here it comes finally to ground—reference to one basic facet of human nature and to one subordinate to it. The former is an impulse, reflected constantly though diffusely in all of man's works, to define himself in terms of process, in both its order and its openness, in effect *to be* himself; the second impulse, by which the first is made operative, is one which seeks exemplifications of the process so central to him, to find his way through them to the *possibility* of being himself. In a sense the former underwrites all human projects as a tautology: man "tries" to be himself. I have been claiming, however, that those projects of his by which he makes that effort lie at varying distances from their center and that, of them, art comes closest to that center. Plato, in the *Republic*, describes the tyrant as an individual so caught by a process which creates new need as it satisfies old ones that he is doomed to serve the process, not the other way round. The drive for presentational order intrinsic to man, his attempt continually to assert the integrity and wholeness of himself and that which he encounters, is such another tyrant—malevolent, on the one hand, in the sense that it brooks no escape; yet, on the other hand, candid and open: it makes no pretensions of being other than it is. Art is the primary means by which man strives at once to placate and to transcend this force; it provides for its audience devices they could not have contrived for themselves with which to find the presentational order which is necessary not just aesthetically, but humanly. It is in this vein that Hegel writes, looking to the core of his reflections on art, that "man possesses an impulse to assert himself in that which is presented him in immediacy, in that which is at hand as an external something to himself, and by doing so at the same time once more to recognize himself therein." [10] Thus appears a final, confirming irony of the doctrine usually named aestheticism—the doctrine that looks to art as an escape from the self, when it is precisely the self that the viewer will encounter there, more determinately and more assertively than anywhere else.

It may seem that the stress on process in this account flattens art and its experience into a single and narrow, almost traditionally formal, dimension. But this would be the case only if the account held that the variables which affected the media of art were restricted to one-dimensional models of presentational order such as that marked by the hour hand of a clock. In fact, the range of art's process is considerably more expansive; the impulse for it and in response to it functions in a world of media and transactions populated by meanings as well as by shapes and colors. The parameters which presentational order may incorporate, attached to such various elements as numbers, words, sounds, are indefinitely numerous. The arts as we already know them have touched a startling variety among these parameters, and there is no reason for assuming that innovation in the media of art is at an end; the expressive accomplishments of art which are already facts drawn out of this variety themselves suggest the possibility of other parameters and meanings. Certainly the realization in which any particular art work concludes is not simply another point in the common sequence of points to which that work by analysis might be reduced. The realization of this, and so the realization of art as an enterprise, spreads backward and forward and sideways, perhaps not indefinitely, but largely.

To set for art the conditions of intentionality in presentational order, then, is not to assign a character which by its generality simply swallows art whole. It is true that as a ground, the impulses for the aesthetic moment also make other appearances. But the place of art with respect to those impulses is distinctive. In some sense, the order of art faces them more forthrightly and deliberately than any other human project: it does not attempt to use or mitigate them, as technology does; it does not attempt to detach itself and to understand the objects of art as objects, in the manner of science. Art asks *to be* that order: it is thus at once condemned to futility—and yet, still, is invited by both the viewer and the creator as a means. The tensions from which it emerges and which it continues to embody or represent account both for the rich multiplicity of art's forms in the past and its prospect on the future. The death of art has been proclaimed too often to allow us either to credit any particular claim or to ignore the possibility. If it has not occurred quite at the time and in the manner predicted by Hegel, for example, it may yet. But should this occur, it will reflect a fundamental change in the human nature of which art was, at another time, an integral part. Given man as he now is and acts, the impossibility of what art and the aesthetic vision attempt to accomplish is a persistent irony; in the absence of the phenomenon of art the attempt itself would hardly be conceivable. It is precisely in the continuing response to a present question—contingent though it be—that art's creativity, and thus man's, appears.

Postscript: Aesthetics and Metaphysics

It will be evident that sections of chapter 5 have carried the attempt at aesthetic inquiry over the boundary between it and metaphysics—a condition of both aesthetics and metaphysics predicted in the first essay of this sequence. The formal justification for such trespassing is simple enough: that to identify or to reconstruct the features of a class of objects or moments of experience requires categories which apply both to the class and beyond it. Ideally—at the end to which they ordinarily no more than reach—such categories or modes of explanation would be perfectly general. The attempt to achieve understanding in the absence of such comprehensiveness could possibly succeed; intuition, after all, has resources of its own. More than likely, however, its results must remain merely idiosyncratic.

The derivation of the categories invoked above, for example, in the Modes of Articulation and in the reference of intentionality to its conditions, is not itself strictly a project for aesthetics; nor has it been undertaken here on the systematic scale that would be expected of a fully formed metaphysics, although assumptions have been made both as to how the latter would proceed and what conclusions it would reach. This limitation is not due merely to my reluctance to confront here the larger issues. The abstractions of metaphysics, if they are to have any point, must originate in and answer to experience in its individual moments and types. And it is from this side of the process which *leads* to metaphysics, specifically from the aesthetic source, that the present discussion has moved.

The restrictions on what has been undertaken, however,

define quite explicitly what is required if its conclusions are to be validated more generally. The excursion made into metaphysics reflects primarily on evidence afforded by the aesthetic datum; and it has proceeded with the hope that in construing the distinctions between aesthetic objects and aesthetic experience, on the one hand, and objects and experience in general, on the other, the definition of the latter has been substantiated, not simply prejudiced by the evidence cited in support of the distinction. But finally there is no way of being assured of this, or—if prejudice *has* been at work—of correcting it, without comparing it to analyses similar to this one for each of the other significant varieties of data. If, in other words, the categories utilized in metaphysical reconstruction are to be both general and apposite, they must have the whole of experience as a sounding board: to do metaphysics as it ought to be done is to omit nothing at all, either at its source or at the end against which it must be measured. This fact, although it does not justify whatever bias has skewed the present account, indicates a remedy which I have not even pretended to supply. The attempt has been made here to look philosophically at one of the many sides of experience, and, in doing this, to provide an understanding of it and a foothold on that larger landscape which metaphysics as a whole must traverse. The test, then, will finally be in the measure of that larger understanding.

A second demurrer, foreshadowed in the opening chapter and active since, is also worth noting in its consequences for the attempt here to relate aesthetics and metaphysics. No claim has been made of demonstrating the subject matter of aesthetics for which understanding has been sought. The reasons for this will, by this point, be all too evident. The discussion moved first from evidence which reflects the existence of art—the practice of criticism—and concluded in speculation on what could have produced that evidence. Art or the aesthetic moment, although at issue, has nowhere itself appeared. Even the citations of particular works of art have been beside the fact: they have been adduced as examples or indicators. But this, I should insist, is an accurate reflection on the character of aesthetic (and philosophical) inquiry. The question is not whether the fact of art *could* have been demonstrated here, but how doing so would have found a place in the process of analysis. Clearly enough, to give an account of a phenomenon is different from either producing or exhibiting the phenomenon; and even if the possibility of the one assumes the actuality of the other, the projects are conceptually separable.

The latter claim gains in force as we note its tacit presence in the question of how is the aesthetic moment possible? That question, I suggested in the early stages of the discussion, affords an easy summary of the form of aesthetics and of the kind of question to which it must answer. And in it, the fact of aesthetic experience, although, on Kant's distinction, only thought, not known, is to that extent taken for granted. The reason why such a move does not beg the question, why the circle which it apparently completes is not vicious, is that the procedure inspired by the assumption is open to a constant, and at least quasi-independent check. Finally, the answer to the question of how the aesthetic moment is possible must answer to the aesthetic moment.

Other internal aspects of that same question are more problematic still, especially as concerns the conception of possibility which it employs. I can at this point only reiterate what I have understood by that term and what this understanding signifies in the process of philosophical explanation which has been followed. The search here has been for a ground of explication, for concepts on the basis of which the appearance of certain phenomena could be discriminated and made intelligible. This is to say something more than that the concepts derived have been intended only to be consistent with the phenomena, or merely possible. It signifies not only possibility but probability— that the concepts, even allowing that they, like the phenomena, are not necessary, yet somehow reconstitute the phenomena in a way which is responsive at once to the concrete quality of the phenomena and to any of the abstract explanatory frameworks which might positively be applied to them. I know no other means of formulating this last stage of philosophical explanation;

its vagaries, if not excused, are made quite plain by the fact that, finally, explanation is self-referential: we must be in a position to employ it in order to understand it.

The confluence of aesthetics and metaphysics, it may be noted, implies no loss of identity for either of them or for the aesthetic moment either. It means only that their status is defined functionally—that the understanding to which they lead emerges as the demands on each are met in conjunction with the demands on the other—and that as this condition is satisfied, a synthesis may be possible which concludes in a new quality of attention both towards the moment which serves as stimulus and, by way of reflection, for other moments as well. I have attempted, from the side of the empirical evidence rooted in the phenomenon of art, to make the phenomenon speak for itself, primarily as its voice is heard in critical judgment; this would, I have assumed, establish the substantive interest and formal limits of the analysis. The attempt from the other side has been to deploy categories sufficiently general to account for that particularity, to identify it with respect to other objects or moments, as well as with respect to other categories. The tests of the conclusions reached come also from two directions. One of these concerns the applicability of the conclusions to the objects and situations they purportedly represent—whether what has been said holds in fact, wherever the facts touch; the other asks after the coherence or internal consistency of the concepts and relations registered in the account of that concrete surface.

The latter criteria contain in their generality no temporal parameters. But the material which serves them as subject obviously does; thus, neither the explication of the aesthetic moment nor the abstraction of categories which purportedly respond to it can reasonably assume, let alone prove, that their projects are, at any point, completed. Philosophy as an enterprise, even the applied philosophy of aesthetics, is certainly not art. But given the evidence for the existence of art or, more generally, of the aesthetic moment, the work and method of philosophy cannot avoid taking that existence into account or attempting to provide an account for it. There are a large number of sources which invite philosophical inquiry, insuring by their own character, its open and dialectical structure; among them, the locus of aesthetic experience is significant. Any of those sources may alter; this feature of contingency, in fact and in prospect, will necessarily recur in the conclusions of inquiry. A reminder, at once factual and symbolic, from the world we address, that philosophy is, after all, a human project.

Notes

Chapter 1

1. *Mind* 67 (1958): 317–34. See the related criticism of Marshall Cohen, "Aesthetic Essence," in *Philosophy in America*, ed. Max Black (Ithaca, 1965); Beryl Lake, "A Study of the Irrefutability of Two Aesthetic Theories," in *Aesthetics and Language*, ed. William Elton (Oxford, 1954): 100–13; Morris Weitz, "The Role of Theory in Aesthetics," *Journal of Aesthetics and Art Criticism* 15 (1956): 27–35; George Dickie, *Aesthetics* (1971), pp. 41 ff. Most of these recent accounts derive from Wittgenstein's work on the fallacies which (allegedly) occur in "traditional" conceptions of linguistic usage and naming (see, e.g., *The Blue Book* [Oxford, 1958], pp. 19–20; *The Brown Book* [Oxford, 1958], pp. 129 ff; *Philosophical Investigations*, secs. 65–76). (As clear a statement as any on the nature of such fallacies appears in the work of the philosopher most often accused of having been victimized by them: See Plato's *Statesman* 262 D *ff.*) For variations on the position taken here, see Monroe C. Beardsley, "The Definition of the Arts," *JAAC* 20 (1961): 175–87; J. N. Findlay, "The Perspicuous and the Poignant," *British Journal of Aesthetics* 7 (1967): 3–19; G. Wolandt, "Über Recht und Grenzen einer subjektstheoretischer Ästhetik," *Jahrbuch für Ästhetik und allgemeine Kunstwissenschaft* 9 (1964): 28–48; Mikel Dufrenne, "L'Apport de l'Esthetique à la Philosophie," in *Esthetique et Philosophie* (Paris, 1967); Karl Aschenbrenner, "The Philosopher's Interest in the Arts," *Journal of Aesthetic Education* 5 (1971): 11–22.
2. Kennick's suggestion that we determine what works of art are (and what objects *are* works of art) by rules of common usage does not answer this objection. Unless he also means to say that such rules are arbitrary or systematically ambiguous, the reason for their "common usage" can only be that they refer in some way to features in the objects they designate. This point qualifies as well the classification of works of art in terms of "family resemblance": unless we know, to begin with, the "natural" limits of the family—a family name—family resemblance could hardly distinguish one object or group of objects from any other. Compare the related criticism of Maurice Mandelbaum, "Family Resemblances and Generalization Concerning the Arts," *American Philosophical Quarterly* 2 (1965): 219–28.
3. Benedetto Croce, *Guide to Aesthetics*, trans. Patrick Romanell (Indianapolis, 1955).
4. One important example of this confusion in systems of aesthetics is the tendency to derive the problems of art and the categories which apply to them from one (group) of the arts. It is clear, for example, that Roger Fry's aesthetic categories

211

respond most immediately to painting and especially to the abstract painting for which he was an early advocate; that Langer's writings derive principally from a concern with music, and Santayana's from literature. This kind of predisposition may be unavoidable; it may also, in any particular case, turn out all to the good. But it suggests an obvious danger of parochialism for theories which purport to speak of art in general.

5. Cf. on the basis of such attempts Ernest Nagel, "Teleological Explanation and Teleological Systems," in *Vision and Action: Essays in Honor of Horace Kallen on His Seventieth Birthday*, ed. Sidney Ratner (New Brunswick, N. J., 1953). For an older paradigm of this attempt, see Hobbes, *Elements of Philosophy Concerning Body*, "Of Power and Act," chap. 10, sec. 7.

6. See *Metaphysics*, 988a17 *ff.*

7. See Carl Hempel, *Aspects of Scientific Explanation* (New York, 1965), pp. 412–15; Israel Scheffler, *The Anatomy of Inquiry* (New York, 1963), pp. 31–43. For criticisms of the covering-law model, see, for instance, Alan Donagan, "The Popper-Hempel Theory," in *Philosophical Analysis and History*, ed. William Dray (New York, 1966), and William Dray, *Laws and Explanation in History* (Oxford, 1957), chap. 5.

8. Attempts have been made, of course, to represent aesthetics as a first-order science, for example, in Fechner's attempt to establish it as a branch of psychology (and finally, by implication, of physiology). A decision on this classification, while it may be in some measure conventional, is not arbitrary: the question finally is whether psychology (or any like first-order science) does in fact provide all the understanding we require of the "facts" of art. My thesis here is that it does not—or at least that it has not—and for good reason.

9. This "follows" has inductive, not deductive force. The arguments raised against a deductive version of the covering-law model (see Dray, *Laws and Explanation in History*, and "On Explaining How Possibly," *The Monist* 52 [1968]: 390–407) seem to me conclusive, if only, as Dray points out, because to adhere strictly to the deductive model suggests the impossibility of explanation at all. This qualification reiterates the stress on the covering-law model as a model of intelligibility or understanding, not specifically (although still possibly) as a predictive or causal model.

10. I follow here Hempel's account of the law-like character of genetic explanation (pp. 447*ff*). This is not yet to confront the question as to how the general principles by which the "causes" effect their explanation are derived; and surely that is an important omission for an argument which takes a model of scientific explanation to be pertinent for philosophical explanation. This problem is faced more directly in chapter 5.

11. On this point see E. M. Bartlett, "The Determination of the Aesthetic Minimum," *Proceedings of the Aristotelian Society* 25 (1934–35): 116 *ff.*

12. See Whitehead's account of criteria of adequacy in *Process and Reality* (New York, 1929), pt. 1, chap. 1, titled "Speculative Philosophy."

Chapter 2

1. See, for example, statements such as that in C. L. Stevenson, *Ethics and Language*

(New Haven, 1944), p. 210: "The purport of the persuasive definition is to alter the descriptive meaning of the term, usually by giving it greater precision within the boundaries of its customary vagueness; but the definition does not make any substantial change in the term's emotive meaning. And the definition is used, consciously or unconsciously, in an effort to secure . . . a redirection of people's attitudes."

2. See the Second Introduction to the *Critique of Judgment*, Section 4. Note also Kant's distinction between determinant and reflective judgment which is applied in what follows here as the "reflective" mode of criticism. (See also the parallel use of the concept in Ronald S. Crane, *The Idea of the Humanities* [Chicago, 1967], vol. 2: "Criticism as Inquiry.") This usage of the term "rule" may be questioned, for example, in its applicability to the historical statements of syntactic judgment. The rule in such cases (for example, in identifying Peter among the Apostles) is comprised of the evidence available, aside from the painting, about Peter; the syntactic conclusion or judgment follows from the application of the rule(s) to the painted figures. On the status of syntactic judgment, see W. K. Wimsatt, "Explication as Criticism," in his *Explication as Criticism* (New York, 1963).

3. *Principia Ethica* (Cambridge, 1903), chap. 6.

4. It might be objected that generic divisions in art *do* bear on the import of works of art—for example, that the short story is an inadequate medium for tragedy. Unquestionably, some connection exists between the medium of the work of art and its message; all that I claim is that they are not identical.

5. This claim may seem rather too easy a dismissal of the significant thesis, for instance, of Valéry, that it is a feature of the work of art to be a fragment and not a whole or unity at all. But the latter position principally wishes to underscore the reverberation of the art work beyond its formal bounds; there is no incompatibility between that intent and the claim made here that the critical impulse is to grasp all that there is to be grasped of the work of art and that that constitutes a unity no matter how that grasp is consequently absorbed or reapplied.

6. Lionel Trilling, "Little Dorrit," reprinted in *The Opposing Self* (New York, 1955), p. 64.

7. Rudolf Wittkower, *Bernini* (London, 1955), p. 11.

8. For a review of these attempts, see C. G. Hempel, "Empiricist Criteria of Cognitive Significance: Problems and Changes," reprinted in *Aspects of Scientific Explanation* (cited above, chap. 1, note 7).

9. This is a bald statement of a large problem in the theory of perception. At least one account, that of the Gestaltists, is apparently at odds with it; and it makes not even the pretense of dealing with the question of how, for any particular reflective judgment, its principles or rules are derived in fact. The unargued premise of my account may be less objectionable than these points suggest—namely (and only) that some patterns of perception or intelligibility develop as a function of experience. This implies neither a psychological atomism nor a private language as some critics of the thesis assume (see, for instance, Rush Rhees, "Can There Be a Private Language?" *Proceedings of the Aristotelian Society*, suppl. vol. 28 [1954]: 77–94).

10. The original and most influential of the contemporary statements is in A. J. Ayer, *Language, Truth, and Logic* (London, 1936), chap. 6. Not that Ayer's position was without its own precedents. (As an example, see Hobbes's *Leviathan*, pt. 1, chap. 6.)

11. This point is made in a number of modified versions of the emotivist position and in Ayer's introduction to the second edition (1946) of *Language, Truth, and Logic* (pp. 20 ff.). See also R. M. Hare, *The Language of Morals* (Oxford, 1952), chap. 6; J. O. Urmson, "On Grading," reprinted in *Logic and Language*, ed. Anthony Flew, 2d ser. (Oxford, 1959).

12. Frank Sibley in his essay on "Aesthetic Concepts," *Philosophical Review* 68 (1959): 421–50; and in his follow-up essay, also in *Philosophical Review*: "Aesthetic and Non-Aesthetic," 74 (1965): 135–59, grants this point—and in doing so undermines his own distinction between "aesthetic" and "non-aesthetic" concepts. Sibley's thesis includes the claim that nobody can be argued into feeling aesthetic qualities. But I know of no theory of art which has taken that position. The more pertinent questions are whether, on the basis of certain empirical, "non-aesthetic" data, one can make any inferences about the experience which they are likely to sponsor and whether the critical eye itself operates in an analogous manner.

13. There can be little point in rehearsing the voluminous literature inspired by Moore's formulation of the "Naturalistic Fallacy"; the reader is referred for the reaction at work here to the essay by Berel Lang and Gary Stahl, "Mill's 'Howlers' and the Logic of Naturalism," *Philosophy and Phenomenological Research* 29 (1969): 562–74.

14. On the background to this question see especially W. V. Quine, "Two Dogmas of Empiricism," in his *From a Logical Point of View* (Cambridge, Mass., 1953).

15. I have in mind in this connection the work of J. L. Austin, in his essays "Performative-Constative," in *Philosophy and Ordinary Language*, ed. Charles Caton (Urbana, 1963), "Other Minds" and "Performative Utterances," in *Philosophical Papers* (Oxford, 1961), and in his William James Lectures, *How To Do Things With Words* (Cambridge, Mass., 1962). Margaret MacDonald's essay "Some Distinctive Features of Arguments Used in Criticism of the Arts," *Proceedings of the Aristotelian Society*, suppl. vol. 33 (1949) sees a connection between critical judgment and performatives, although she draws different and, in fact, conflicting conclusions to the ones drawn here. T. R. Martland in "Austin, Art, and Anxiety," *JAAC* 29 (1970): 169–74 hints at the possibility that the performance as construed by Austin may describe the creative process.

16. These limits to the art work are not those which the artist ascribes to it. At the point at which the artist begins to reflect on his work, he gives up the license which his art allows him. Even having created it, he may not know or be able to articulate all of what his work contains; he may also attribute to it properties which it lacks. In short, he is a critic. See on this point W. K. Wimsatt and Monroe C. Beardsley, "The Intentional Fallacy," reprinted in W. K. Wimsatt, *The Verbal Icon* (Lexington, Ky., 1956), and the more moderate statements, which nonetheless agree with the central thesis of Wimsatt and Beardsley, by Henry Aiken, "The Aesthetic Relevance of Artists' Intentions," *Journal of Philosophy* 52 (1955): 742–53; Isabel Hungerland, "The Concept of Intention in Art Criticism," *Journal of Philosophy* 52 (1955): 733–42; Richard Kuhns, "Criticism and the Problem of Intention," *Journal of Philosophy* 57 (1960): 5–23; Monroe C. Beardsley, *The Possibility of Criticism* (Detroit, 1970), chap. 1; and George Dickie, *Aesthetics*, pp. 110–21. This is one issue in aesthetics, I think, which requires no more arguing—which is not to say that it will not continue to be mistaken; see, for example, E. D. Hirsch, *Validity in Interpretation* (New Haven, 1967).

Chapter 3

1. For emphasis on the fault of art or the artist rather than of the audience, see N. R. Murphy, *The Interpretation of Plato's Republic* (Oxford, 1951), chap. 11; R. C. Lodge, *Plato's Theory of Art* (London, 1953), chap. 14. For a fuller exposition of the interpretation given here (but *just* for his exposition of Plato's concept of art), see E. A. Havelock, *Preface to Plato* (Oxford, 1963), chaps. 1 and 2.
2. A move which Kant himself had foreshadowed—as it were, against himself—with his doctrine of Aesthetic Ideas and the symbolic force of beauty.
3. Bertrand Russell, "On Denoting," *Mind*, n.s. 14 (1905): 479–93.
4. See, for instance, Gilbert Ryle, " 'If,' 'So,' and 'Because,' " in *Philosophical Analysis*, ed. Max Black (Ithaca, 1950). See also Nelson Goodman's attempt, in *Languages of Art* (Indianapolis, 1968), to show how, contrary to Russell, art can be representational without denoting at all. Goodman seems to suggest even that a work as a whole can "metaphorically" denote although none of its components is denotative (p. 85). There is considerable strain in both of these theses because Goodman shares a premise of Russell's—that if a portrait denotes, it denotes only the historical personage portrayed—but wishes to avoid Russell's emphasis on the falsity of art's denotation. But why accept the premise?
5. A classic case, but not without its own classical precedent. Sir Philip Sidney's reply to the Puritan attacks on the arts in *A Defense of Poesie*, that the poet "nothing affirms and therefore never lieth," takes the same form. For Richards's position, see *Science and Poetry* (New York, 1926) and *Principles of Literary Criticism* (New York, 1938), pp. 261 *ff*.
6. See Margaret Macdonald, "The Language of Fiction," *Proceedings of the Aristotelian Society* 28 (1954): 165–84; R. G. Collingwood, *The Principles of Art* (Oxford, 1938), pp. 264 *ff*; Max Black, "Some Questions about Emotive Meaning," *Philosophical Review*, 57 (1948); Alan Tormey, *The Concept of Expression* (Princeton, 1970), pp. 63–68.
7. Isenberg makes much—too much—of this point. (See "The Problem of Belief," *JAAC* 13, 1955.) "What is so glorious," he asks, "about truth?"—a rhetorical question, in his reckoning, which warrants more than a rhetorical answer.
8. A related approach to the analysis of the cognitive status of literature has been suggested by John Hospers, "Implied Truths in Literature," *JAAC* 19 (1960): 37–47; see also Theodore Greene, *The Arts and the Art of Criticism* (Princeton, 1940); Morris Weitz, *The Philosophy of the Arts* (Cambridge, Mass., 1950), chap. 8. For a statement of a position close to Richards's which is more attentive to the systematic question of denotation, consult Jercy Pelc, "Nominal Expressions and Literary Fiction," trans. O. Wojtasiewicz from *Studia Estetygene* 4 (1967): 317–36 and privately circulated.
9. "The Communication of the Word," in *Emily Dickinson*, ed. R. B. Sewall (Englewood Cliffs, N. J., 1963), p. 66.
10. *Art as Experience* (New York, 1934), pp. 110 ff. Dewey enlarges here on a suggestion of A. C. Bradley in "Poetry for Poetry's Sake," in *Oxford Lectures on Poetry* (London, 1907).
11. For an account which moves in the same direction that this one does, although with substantial differences in detail, cf. the conclusion to Volume I of Roman

Ingarden's *Studia & Estetyki* (Warsaw, 1966). One of the points Ingarden makes is especially pertinent to the position taken here—that if their "literal" denotation is distinguished from the aesthetic force of (groups of) sentences, the critic is responsible for knowing which of the two contexts he is treating. A repeated instance of the confusion of these contexts has arisen in connection with the statement "Beauty is truth, truth beauty," which commentators on Keats' "Ode" often assume to be the implication of the poem, ignoring the fact that it is not the poem that makes the declaration but as the poem ascribes it the Grecian Urn. So far as an understanding of the ode is concerned, then, the line must be viewed as one among a number of items which are to be interpreted. See on this point also Tormey, *The Concept of Expression*, p. 158.

12. Cleanth Brooks, *The Well Wrought Urn* (New York, 1947), chap. 11. Brooks's is one formulation among many in the history of aesthetics which argue that to change even the slightest feature of a work of art, and certainly to reformulate the whole, is to be faced with an essentially different object from the original. (See, for example, Etienne Gilson, *Painting and Reality*, [New York, 1959], chap. 3.) The fact remains that in a strict sense, this argument is valid not only for works of art, but for any object at all; it is a reformulation of Leibniz's Principle of the Identity of Indiscernibles. To question the use of this principle does not mean that it is not relevant to the art work, only that it is not peculiarly relevant there; and that the emphasis on it with respect to art has thus been conceptually misleading. Many things can be "done" to a work of art which, while they may detract from the original and while, strictly speaking, they change it, do not raise questions about the changed identity or value of the work, except perhaps in those works which are extraordinarily sparse to begin with, such as the seventeen-syllable poems of Haiku. The *Venus de Milo* may not be admired because she has no arms, but it is not at all clear that she would be more (or more deservedly) admired if her arms should be found.

13. See especially, among many writings of these authors, Wolfgang Köhler and D. F. H. Wallach, "Figural After-effects: An Investigation of Visual Processes," *Proceedings of the American Philosophical Society* 88 (1944): 269–357; K. S. Lashley, "The Mechanism of Vision," *Journal of General Psychology* 18 (1938): 123–93.

14. On this metaphor, see E. H. Gombrich, "Illusion and Visual Deadlock," in *Meditations on a Hobby Horse* (London, 1963), pp. 155–56, and J. J. Gibson, "The Information Available in Pictures," *Leonardo*, 4 (1971): 27–35.

15. See *The Collected Papers of C. S. Peirce* (Cambridge, 1931), 2.247; C. W. Morris, *Signs, Language, and Behavior* (Englewood Cliffs, N. J., 1946), chaps. 5 and 7.

16. This point does not bear necessarily (although it may in fact) on the comparative value of the arts. Empirical evidence for a thesis contrasting the relative complexity of syntactic elements in different media would presuppose work in the psychology of art which, so far as I can determine, has not yet been done. This would include, as an example, tracing differences in memory capability with respect to objects in different media.

17. As represented, for example, in such works as Robert Peterson, *The Art of Ecstasy* (New York, 1970), and Mario Praz, *Mnemosyne: The Parallel between Literature and the Visual Arts* (Princeton, 1970). See also the introduction to E. H. Gombrich, *Norm and Form* (London, 1966), and, for an extension to the denotation of "natural art works" (such as parks, gardens), Paul Shepard, *Man in the Landscape: A*

Historic View of the Esthetics of Nature (New York, 1967), chap. 3. On the limitations of such parallelisms, see Meyer Shapiro, "Style," in *Aesthetics Today*, ed. Morris Philipson (New York, 1961) pp. 91–92.

18. For accounts of art as (traditionally) representational or symbolic, see, for instance, Morris, *Signs, Language, and Behavior*, and Susanne K. Langer, *Philosophy in a New Key* (Cambridge, Mass., 1942); and the common critical theme, against such efforts, of Richard Rudner, "On Semiotic Aesthetics," *JAAC* 10 (1951): 67–77; Max Black, "The Semiotic of Morris," in his *Language and Philosophy* (Ithaca, 1949); and Berel Lang, "Langer's Arabesque and the Collapse of the Symbol," *Review of Metaphysics* 16 (1962): 349–65.

Chapter 4

1. For instance, Edward Bullough, " 'Psychical Distance' as a Factor in Art and an Aesthetic Principle," *British Journal of Psychology* 5 (1912), reprinted in *Aesthetics* (Stanford, 1957); Sheila Dawson, "Distancing as an Aesthetic Principle," *Australian Journal of Philosophy* 39: 155–74; Eliseo Vivas, "Literature and Knowledge," in *Creation and Discovery* (New York, 1955).

2. The strength of the foundation is attested even in much of the criticism that has been directed against the concept of disinterest, which often seems to circle back in its conclusions towards some version of that concept. See, for instance, J. O. Urmson, "What Makes a Situation Aesthetic?" *Proceedings of the Aristotelian Society* 31 (1957): 75–92, and George Dickie, "The Myth of the Aesthetic Attitude," *American Philosophical Quarterly* 1 (1964): 56–65; Richard Wollheim, *Art and Its Objects* (New York, 1968), sec. 40 ff.

3. *An Inquiry Concerning Beauty*, reprinted in *Aesthetic Theories*, ed. Karl Aschenbrenner and Arnold Isenberg (Englewood Cliffs, N. J., 1965), p. 84.

4. See, for instance, in the *Critique of Judgment*, secs. 29, 34, and 40 for explicit references; the evidence of tacit influence is more difficult to demonstrate, but is nonetheless clear. For the historical background on the issue, see Ernst Cassirer, *The Philosophy of the Enlightenment* (Princeton, 1951); Alfred Baeumler, *Das Irrationalitätsproblem in der Ästhetik und Logik des 18. Jahrhunderts* (Halle, 1923), chaps. 1–7; and Jerome Stolnitz, "On the Origins of Aesthetic Disinterestedness," *JAAC*, 20 (1961): 161–83. Saisselin argues that the principal source of Kant's work was French rather than English (see *Taste in Eighteenth Century France* [Syracuse, 1965], chaps. 1 and 9); but he proves no more, it seems, than that the concepts had appeared in different places—which is true and not only for eighteenth-century France. See F. J. Kovach, *"Die Ästhetik das Thomas von Aquin"* (Berlin, 1961), pp. 198 ff; and, well before that, Plato's *Symposium*, 205 *ff*; *Philebus*, pp. 52, 65.

5. For example, in such a passage: "But that the reference to delight is wholly different where what gratifies is at the same time called *good*, is evident from the fact that with the good the question always is whether it is mediately or immediately good, i.e., useful or good in itself; whereas with the agreeable this point can never arise, since the word always means what pleases immediately—and it is the same with what I call beautiful." (*Critique of Aesthetic Judgment*, sec. 4.)

6. See Anthony Ashley Cooper, 3rd Earl of Shaftesbury, *Characteristics* (London, 1900), 1: 275; 2: 270.

7. John Dewey, *Art as Experience* (New York, 1934), p. 25. See also Paul Kristeller, "The Modern System of the Arts," *Journal of the History of Ideas* 41 (1952) for an account of the classification (as defining the limits of their extent) of the arts, a different, but related problem.
8. *Characteristics*, pt. 3, sec. 2.
9. *Aesthetics*, p. 100.
10. For instance, Arnold Isenberg in "The Problem of Belief," *JAAC* 13 (1955), who, although arguing against the importance of belief in the aesthetic experience, acknowledges the relevance of extra-aesthetic beliefs (as extra-aesthetic).
11. The most cogent version of this "consequential" analysis of art appears in the work of Marxist writers on the arts (see, for instance, Leon Trotsky, *Literature and Revolution* (Ann Arbor, 1960); Christopher Caudwell, *Illusion and Reality* (London, 1937); Gyorgy Lukàcs, *The Historical Novel* (London, 1962). For a collection of Marxist statements in aesthetics, see Berel Lang and Forrest Williams, eds., *Marxism and Art* (New York, 1972). It is interesting to note that notwithstanding the Marxist emphasis on the social preconditions and consequences of the aesthetic process, a place may be reserved for the phenomenon of disinterest (see Gyorgii Plekhanov, *Art and Society* [New York, 1936]).

Chapter 5

1. The question of the status of animal art is related in an obvious way to the issue raised here. For an intriguing account of some of the empirical data affecting that relation as concerns the birth of art among chimpanzees, see Desmond Morris, *The Biology of Art* (London, 1962).
2. I recognize that the term "intentionality" figures in many and quite different contexts in the recent philosophical literature (for example, among both the phenomenologists and the modal logicians); and that to burden it with another, albeit related, use is to risk confusion. It is important, in particular, to distinguish the usage here from that of Brentano and later of Husserl in their descriptive analysis of intentional objects and acts. The account given here construes aesthetic perception as intentional: Reflective judgment is sustained by, and unintelligible without, its object—the work of art. There is, however, no question either of bracketing the field of intentionality, and thus the work of art and its implications, off from a real background, or of asserting intentionality as a feature of acts or objects in general.

    If the question is one of precedence, the usage employed here has if anything a longer history than the others. Its direct ancestor is the concept of "Zweckmässigkeit," which is of central importance in Kant's *Critique of Judgment*; for a more recent application of the term, see Erwin Panofsky, "Art as a Humanistic Discipline," in *Meaning in the Visual Arts* (Garden City, N. Y., 1957).
3. For references to the discussion of the artist's intention, see chapter 2, note 16, above.
4. See the classical work on the "aesthetics of nature" of D'Arcy Thompson, *On Growth and Form* (Cambridge, Eng., 1942). The most important philosophical attempt to face up to this issue remains Kant's conjunction of the *Critique of Aesthetic Judgment* and the *Critique of Teleological Judgment*.
5. See G. E. M. Anscombe, *Intention* (Ithaca, 1962), pp. 9 *ff.*
6. I borrow the term "presentational" from Susanne Langer's use in *Philosophy in a*

New Key (Cambridge, 1942), although with modification of the sharp line Langer draws between the presentational and the discursive symbol.

7. E. H. Gombrich's *Art and Illusion* (New York, 1961) provides independent testimony to the pertinence of these components, in the conception of art history as "making and matching." Gombrich's analysis is primarily stylistic in focus, intended to provide a key to the history of artistic vision (literally, since he concentrates on the visual arts). But the form he assigns that history, in the repeated movement from what is first given to the consequent discovery of vision, approximates in historical development what I have ascribed here to the individual moment.

8. See Albert Hofstadter's comments "Concerning a Certain Dewyan Conception of Metaphysics," in *John Dewey*, ed. Sidney Hook (New York, 1950) which argues this point in greater detail.

9. For a number of aspects of this account, I have drawn on Hofstadter's *Truth and Art* (New York, 1965). See also my review of that book, "Aesthetic Inquiry and Art's Body," in *Journal of Philosophy* 67 (1970): 986–94.

10. *The Introduction to Hegel's Philosophy of Fine Art*, trans. Bernard Bosanquet, reprinted in *G. W. F. Hegel on Art, Religion, Philosophy*, ed. J. G. Gray (New York, 1970), p. 58.

Bibliography

Aiken, Henry. "The Aesthetic Relevance of Artists' Intentions." *Journal of Philosophy* 52 (1955): 742–53.

Anscombe, G. E. M. *Intention*. Ithaca, 1962.

Aristotle, *The Works of*. Edited by W. D. Ross. Oxford, 1910–52.

Aschenbrenner, Karl. "The Philosopher's Interest in the Arts," *Journal of Aesthetic Education* 5 (1971): 11–22.

Austin, J. L. "Other Minds." In *Philosophical Papers*. Oxford, 1961.

———. *How To Do Things With Words*. Cambridge, Mass., 1962.

———. "Performative-Constative." In Charles E. Caton, ed., *Philosophy and Ordinary Language*. Urbana, 1963.

———. "Performative Utterances." In J. L. Austin, *Philosophical Papers*. Oxford, 1961.

Ayer, A. J. *Language, Truth, and Logic*. 2nd ed. Oxford, 1946.

Baeumler, Alfred. *Das Irrationalitätsproblem in der Ästhetik und Logik des 18. Jahrhunderts*. Halle, 1923.

Bartlett, E. M. "The Determination of the Aesthetic Minimum." *Proceedings of the Aristotelian Society* 25 (1934–35).

Beardsley, Monroe C. "The Definition of the Arts." *JAAC* 20 (1961): 173–87.

———. *The Possibility of Criticism*. Detroit, 1970.

——— and W. K. Wimsatt. "The Intentional Fallacy." Reprinted in W. K. Wimsatt, *The Verbal Icon*. Lexington, Ky., 1956.

Black, Max. "Some Questions About Emotive Meaning." *Philosophical Review* 57 (1948): 111–26.

———. "The Semiotic of Morris." In *Language and Philosophy*. Ithaca, 1949.

Bradley, A. C. "Poetry for Poetry's Sake." In *Oxford Lectures on Poetry*. London, 1907.

Brooks, Cleanth. *The Well Wrought Urn*. New York, 1947.

Bullough, Edward. " 'Psychical Distance' as a Factor in Art and an Aesthetic Principle." *British Journal of Psychology* 5 (1912). Reprinted in *Aesthetics*. Stanford, 1957.

Caudwell, Christopher. *Illusion and Reality*. London, 1937.

Cassirer, Ernst. *The Philosophy of the Enlightenment*. Princeton, 1951.

Cohen, Marshall. "Aesthetic Essence." In *Philosophy in America*, ed. Max Black. Ithaca, 1965.

Collingwood, R. G. *The Principles of Art*. Oxford, 1938.

221

Bibliography

Crane, Ronald S. *The Idea of the Humanities*. Chicago, 1967.

Cooper, Anthony Ashley, 3rd Earl of Shaftesbury. *Characteristics*. London, 1900.

Dawson, Sheila. "Distancing as an Aesthetic Principle." *Australian Journal of Philosophy*, 39 (1961): 155–74.

Dewey, John. *Art as Experience*. New York, 1934.

Dickie, George. *Aesthetics*. Indianapolis, 1971.

———. "The Myth of the Aesthetic Attitude." *American Philosophical Quarterly* 1 (1964): 56–65.

Donagan, Alan. "The Popper-Hempel Theory," in *Philosophical Analysis and History*, ed. William Dray. New York, 1966.

Dray, William. *Laws and Explanation in History*. Oxford, 1957.

———. "On Explaining How Possibly." *The Monist* 52 (1968): 390–407.

Dufrenne, Michel. "L'Apport de l'esthetique à la philosophie." In *Esthetique et Philosophie*. Paris, 1967.

Findlay, J. N. "The Perspicuous and the Poignant." *British Journal of Aesthetics* 7 (1967): 3–19.

Gibson, J. J. "The Information Available in Pictures." *Leonardo*, 4 (1971): 27–35.

Gilson, Etienne. *Painting and Reality*. New York, 1959.

Gombrich, E. H. *Art and Illusion*. New York, 1961.

———. "Illusion and Visual Deadlock." In *Meditations on a Hobby Horse*. London, 1963.

———. *Norm and Form*. London, 1966.

Goodman, Nelson. *Languages of Art*. Indianapolis, 1968.

Greene, Theodore. *The Arts and the Art of Criticism*. Princeton, 1940.

Hare, R. M. *The Language of Morals*. Oxford, 1952.

Havelock, E. A. *Preface to Plato*. Oxford, 1963.

Hempel, Carl. *Aspects of Scientific Explanation*. New York, 1965.

Hirsch, E. D. *Validity in Interpretation*. New Haven, 1967.

Hobbes, Thomas. *Leviathan*, ed. Michael Oakeshott. Oxford, 1960.

———. *Elements of Philosophy Concerning Body*. In *Selections*, ed. F. J. E. Woodbridge. New York, 1958.

Hofstadter, Albert. "Concerning a Certain Deweyan Conception of Metaphysics." In *John Dewey*, ed. Sidney Hook. New York, 1950.

———. *Truth and Art*. New York, 1965.

Hospers, John. "Implied Truths in Literature." *JAAC* 19 (1960): 37–47.

Hungerland, Isabel. "The Concept of Intention in Art Criticism," *Journal of Philosophy* 52 (1955): 733–42.

Hutcheson, Francis. *An Inquiry Concerning Beauty*. Reprinted in *Aesthetic Theories*, ed. Karl Aschenbrenner and Arnold Isenberg. Englewood Cliffs, N. J., 1965.

Ingarden, Roman. *Studia & Estetyki*. Warsaw, 1966.

Isenberg, Arnold. "The Problem of Belief." *JAAC* 13 (1955): 395–407.

Kant, Immanuel. *Critique of Judgment*, trans. J. H. Bernard. New York, 1951.

Kennick, William. "Does Traditional Aesthetics Rest on a Mistake?" *Mind* 67 (1958): 317–34.

Köhler, Wolfgang and D. F. Holzl Wallach. "Figural After-effects: An Investigation of Visual Processes." *Proceedings of the American Philosophical Society* 88 (1944): 269–357.

Kovach, F. J. *Die Ästhetik das Thomas von Aquin*. Berlin, 1961.

Kresteller, Paul. "The Modern System of the Arts." *Journal of the History of Ideas*, 12–13 (1951–52): 496–527 and 17–47.

Kuhns, Richard. "Criticism and the Problem of Intention." *Journal of Philosophy* 57 (1960): 5–23.

Lake, Beryl. "A Study of the Irrefutability of Two Aesthetic Theories." In *Aesthetics and Language*, ed. William Elton. Oxford, 1954.

Lang, Berel. "Langer's Arabesque and the Collapse of the Symbol." *Review of Metaphysics* 16 (1962): 349–65.

Lang, Berel and Forrest Williams, eds. *Marxism and Art*. New York, 1972.

Lang, Berel and Gary Stahl. "Mill's 'Howlers' and the Logic of Naturalism." *Philosophy and Phenomenological Research* 29 (1969): 562–74.

Langer, Susanne K. *Philosophy in a New Key*. Cambridge, Mass., 1942.

Lashley, K. S. "The Mechanism of Vision," *Journal of General Psychology* 18 (1938): 123–93.

Lodge, R. C. *Plato's Theory of Art*. London, 1953.

Lukàcs, Gyorgy. *The Historical Novel*. London, 1962.

MacDonald, Margaret. "The Language of Fiction." *Proceedings of the Aristotelian Society* 28 (1954): 165–84.

———. "Some Distinctive Features of Arguments Used in Criticism of the Arts." In *Aesthetics and Language*, ed. William Elton. Oxford, 1954. Pp. 114–30.

Mandelbaum, Maurice. "Family Resemblances and Generalization Concerning the Arts." *American Philosophical Quarterly* 2 (1965): 219–28.

Martland, T. R. "Austin, Art, and Anxiety." *JAAC* 29 (1970): 169–74.

Moore, G. E. *Principia Ethica*. Cambridge, 1903.

Morris, C. W. *Signs, Language, and Behavior*. Englewood Cliffs, N. J., 1946.

Morris, Desmond. *The Biology of Art*. London, 1962.

Murphy, N. R. *The Interpretation of Plato's Republic*. Oxford, 1951.

Nagel, Ernest. "Teleological Explanation and Teleological Systems." In *Vision and Action: Essays in Honor of Horace Kallen on His Seventieth Birthday*, ed. Sidney Ratner. New Brunswick, N. J., 1953.

Panofsky, Erwin. "Art as a Humanistic Discipline." In *Meaning in the Visual Arts*. Garden City, N. Y., 1957.

Peirce, C. S. *The Collected Papers of C. S. Peirce*. Cambridge, 1931.

Pelc, J. "Nominal Expressions and Literary Fiction." Trans. O. Wojtasiewicz from *Studia Estetygene* 4 (1967): 317–36 and privately circulated.

Peterson, Robert. *The Art of Ecstasy*. New York, 1970.

Plato. *The Collected Dialogues*, ed. Edith Hamilton and Huntington Cairus. New York, 1961.

Plekhanov, Gyorgii. *Art and Society*. New York, 1936.

Praz, Mario. *Mnemosyne: The Parallel Between Literature and the Visual Arts*. Princeton, 1970.

Quine, Willard Van Orman. "Two Dogmas of Empiricism." In Quine, *From A Logical Point of View*. Cambridge, Mass., 1953.

Rhees, Rush. "Can There Be a Private Language?" *Proceedings of the Aristotelian Society*, suppl. vol. 28 (1954): 77–94.

Richards, I. A. *Principles of Literary Criticism*. New York, 1938.

———. *Science and Poetry*. New York, 1926.

Rudner, Richard. "On Semiotic Aesthetics." *JAAC* 10 (1951): 67–77.

Russell, Bertrand. "On Denoting." *Mind* 14 (1905): 479–93.

Ryle, Gilbert. " 'If,' 'So,' and 'Because.' " In *Philosophical Analysis*, ed. Max Black. Ithaca, 1950.

Saisselin, R. G. *Taste in Eighteenth Century France*. Syracuse, 1965.

Scheffler, Israel. *The Anatomy of Inquiry*. New York, 1963.

Shapiro, Meyer. "Style." In *Aesthetics Today*, ed. Morris Philipson. New York, 1961.

Shepard, Paul. *Man in the Landscape: A Historic View of Esthetics and Nature*. New York, 1967.

Sibley, Frank. "Aesthetic and Non-Aesthetic." *Philosophical Review* 74 (1965): 135–39.

———. "Aesthetic Concepts." *Philosophical Review* 68 (1939): 421–50.

Sidney, Sir Philip. *An Apologie for Poetrie*, ed. E. S. Shuckburg. Cambridge, 1951.

Stevenson, Charles L. *Ethics and Language*. New Haven, 1944.

Stolnitz, Jerome. "On the Origins of Aesthetic Disinterestedness." *JAAC* 20 (1961): 161–83.

Thackrey, Donald. "The Communication of the Word." In *Emily Dickinson*, ed. R. B. Sewall. Englewood Cliffs, N. J., 1963.

Thompson, D'Arcy. *On Growth and Form*. Cambridge, 1942.

Tormey, Alan. *The Concept of Expression*. Princeton, 1970.

Trilling, Lionel. "Little Dorrit." Reprinted in *The Opposing Self*. New York, 1955.

Trotsky, Leon. *Literature and Revolution* (1925). Ann Arbor, 1960.

Urmson, J. O. "On Grading." Reprinted in *Logic and Language*, ed. Anthony Flew. Second series. Oxford, 1959.

———. "What Makes a Situation Aesthetic?" *Proceedings of the Aristotelian Society* 31 (1957): 75–92.

Vivas, Eliseo, "Literature and Knowledge." In *Creation and Discovery*. New York, 1955.

Wallach, D. F. Holzl and Wolfgang Köhler. "Figural After-effects: An Investigation of Visual Processes." *Proceedings of the American Philosophical Society*. 88 (1944): 269–357.

Weitz, Morris. *The Philosophy of the Arts*. Cambridge, 1950.

———. "The Role of Theory in Aesthetics." *JAAC* 15 (1956): 27–35.

Whitehead, Alfred North. *Process and Reality*. New York, 1929.

Wimsatt, William K. "Explication as Criticism." In *Explication as Criticism*. New York, 1963.

——— and Monroe C. Beardsley. "The Intentional Fallacy." Reprinted in W. K. Wimsatt, *The Verbal Icon*. Lexington, Ky., 1956.

Wittgenstein, Ludwig. *The Blue Book*. Oxford, 1958.

———. *The Brown Book*. Oxford, 1958.

———. *Philosophical Investigations*. New York, 1953.

Wittkower, Rudolf. *Bernini*. London, 1955.

Wolandt, G., "Über Recht und Grenzen Einer subjektstheoretischer Ästhetik." *Jahrbuch für Aesthetik und allgemeine Kunstwissenschaft* 9 (1964): 28–48.

Wollheim, Richard. *Art and Its Objects*. New York, 1968.

Index

225

Index

Goodman, Nelson, 100 n.
Gray, J. G., 204 n.
Greene, Theodore, 104 n.

Hanslick, Eduard, 138
Hare, R. M., 66 n.
Hartmann, Victor, 122
Havelock, E. A., 96 n.
Hegel, G. W. F., 37, 97 f., 204 f.
Heidegger, Martin, 97
Hempel, Carl, 26 n., 32 n., 60 n.
Hirsch, E. D., 86 n.
Hobbes, Thomas, 26 n., 65 n.
Hofstadter, Albert, 97, 201 n., 203 n.
Homer, 97
Hospers, John, 104 n.
Hume, David, 19, 98
Hungerland, Isabel, 86 n.
Husserl, Edmund G. A., 176 n.
Hutcheson, Francis, 135 f.

Ingarden, Roman, 97, 111 n.
Isenberg, Arnold, 17, 102 n., 153 n.

Joyce, James, 168, 177 f., 187

Kant, Immanuel, 12, 18, 24, 33, 38 f., 46, 51, 98, 132, 135 ff., 168, 170 ff., 176 n., 177, 178 n., 180, 185, 208
Kazantzakis, Nikos, 110
Keats, John, 83, 111 n., 142
Kennick, William, 18 ff.
Kierkegaard, Sören, 132
Köhler, Wolfgang, 114 n.
Kovach, F. J., 136 n.
Kristeller, Paul, 138 n.
Kuhns, Richard, 86 n.
Kyd, Thomas, 73

Lake, Beryl, 18 n.
Lang, Berel, 71 n., 125 n., 161 n., 203 n.
Langer, Susanne, 23 n., 114, 123, 125 n., 138, 188 n.
Lashley, K. S., 114 n.
Lee, Vernon, 138
Leibniz, Gottfried Wilhelm, 113 n., 136
Lipps, Theodore, 138

Locke, John, 145
Lodge, R. C., 96 n.
Lukàcs, Gyorgy, 97, 161 n.

MacDonald, Margaret, 78 n., 101 n.
McKuen, Rod, 83
Mandelbaum, Maurice, 20 n.
Manet, Edouard, 83
Martland, T. R., 78 n.
Marx, Karl, 196
Masaccio, 117
Meinong, Alexis, 100
Milton, John, 117
Moore, G. E., 11, 54, 71 n.
Morris, C. W., 119 n., 125 n.
Morris, Desmond, 172 n.
Moussorgsky, Modest, 122
Murphy, N. R., 96 n.

Nagel, Ernest, 26 n.

Panofsky, Erwin, 176 n.
Peirce, C. S., 119 n.
Pelc, Jercy, 104 n.
Peterson, Robert, 123 n.
Picasso, Pablo, 49, 111
Plato, 18 n., 19, 23, 25, 94, 96 f., 123, 125 f., 136 n., 161, 196, 203
Plekhanov, Gyorgii, 161 n.
Praz, Mario, 123 n.

Quine, W. V., 77 n.

Respighi, Ottorino, 122
Rhees, Rush, 60 n.
Richards, I. A., 99, 101 ff., 104 n., 138, 142
Rouault, Georges, 66
Rudner, Richard, 125 n.
Russell, Bertrand, 99 ff.
Ryle, Gilbert, 100 n.

Saisselin, R. G., 136 n.
Santayana, George, 17, 23 n., 138
Schapiro, Meyer, 123 n.
Scheffler, Israel, 26 n.
Schiller, F. C. S., 138
Schopenhauer, Arthur, 138
Shaftesbury. See Cooper, Anthony Ashley

226

Berel Lang is professor and former chairman of the Department of Philosophy, at the University of Colorado. He is the coeditor (with Forrest Williams) of Marxism and Art *(New York, 1972).*

The manuscript was prepared for publication by Linda Grant. The book was designed by Julie Paul. The typeface for the text is Caledonia designed by W. A. Dwiggins in 1938; and the display face is Ultra Bodoni.

The text is printed on Nashoba text paper and the book is bound in Joanna Mills' Linson 2, Claret Buckram over flexible binders' boards. Manufactured in the United States of America.